To

____

From

____

On This Date

____

Lang Watson Foundation

The Soul of Our Family

A book of Prayers, Praises, and Poems

The Soul of Our Family

ISBN 978-1-954000-28-5 (paperback)
ISBN 978-1-954000-29-2 (eBook)

Editor: Bob Laning
Cover Design Lead: Raeghan Rebstock

Published 2021 by Publish Authority
300 Colonial Center Parkway, Suite 100
Roswell, GA 30076
www.PublishAuthority.com

Printed in the United States of America

This book is **dedicated** to the memory of our parents, grandparents, great-grand parents and ancestors who taught us that prayer is an indispensable tool to reach GOD during periods of praise as well as difficult times; to our current generation of Lang Watson family members who are challenged with the everyday systemic and institutional racism, economic, and political strife that is consuming our Country and the World; and to future generations so that they too may come to know the power of prayer and meditation in their life, as did their ancestors.

"With long life will I satisfy him, and
shew him my salvation."

Psalms 91:16 King James Version

CONTENTS

FOREWORD

Evangelist Elder Claude Lang and Mother Hazel Natalie Watson Lang are two saints who epitomized sainthood and servitude. They were faithful, loving, caring, anointed, and endowed with God's greatness of having an unchanging love for Him and his people.

After having enormous respect and dedication to God and his Word, the Langs made known the importance of prayer, faith, and praise. There was something about this mixture that would always certainly produce positive results that were pleasing in God's sight. These two servants not only had an immense love for God, his people, and each other, but for their precious family, whom they desired to witness to seeking the Lord with all their might and to be a conduit and catalyst for family members to come. Their love for each other set an example of how it should be done. Praise God it worked! It made an impression on Reverend Dr. David and Delores Blakely's marriage. They were both like spiritual parents to us as role models.

Mother Lang was a church musician and sunshine band leader for 35 years and had a great love for children, even though she had six children of her own.

Delores proceeded Mother Lang as the church musician and sunshine band leader for the next 38 years. She also had the same undeniable love for children. Mother Lang and Evangelist Elder Claude Lang remained spiritual parents for Pastor Elder Dr. David Blakely after his biological father, Bishop William O. Blakely, passed away.

Evangelizing from church to church, city to city, with the message being the same regarding the need for repentance, dedication, prayer, and praise, Elder Lang gave no slack in the fact that it was holiness or hell, and there was no excuse for backsliding. In fact, he said, "Put the slide in front of you and slide forward." He encouraged and preached in-state, out-of-state, and at local churches telling worshipers about the importance of living for God and saying that one did not have to sin. Just live for God, pray, do right, and God will take care of you. He would get righteously indignant when talking about the devil and his antics. Often times he would laugh at what he himself was saying because he was so passionate about what he was saying. There were times when night services were at a close. Congregants were standing, per instructions from their pastor for dismissal, and in would walk Evangelist Elder Claude Lang.

So, the pastor would have to tell the saints to sit back down because Elder Lang was here. What a joy he was, and what monumental moments they were. The general thrust of the message was the same, which was telling us about the importance of being saved, staying saved, praying and praising God, and not giving the devil any space. He would like to kick his leg up high, and we would sit back and be amazed at his ability to do so at his age, with all ease.

He was more than a member, but a spiritual father who loved, prayed for, and honored his spiritual son, Dr. David Blakely, and Mother Delores Blakely. In return, the Pastor and church members honored him by calling him Daddy Lang. The Lang Family and Blakely Family are one family, and that shall always be because we believe it was ordained in heaven to be that way.

Bishop William O. Blakely referred to John Lang the tall one as 'Jeff,' and David Blakely the short one as 'Mutt,' when they were young boys. They have been and always will be best friends and musicians, as well as the other bonds with our other sisters and brothers, nieces and nephews, etc. This is because of the prayers of our spiritual parents that proclaimed them as a must-have. Long live the legacy of prayer and its importance in the fostering of life, hope, and spiritual prosperity in the Lang family.

Reverend Dr. David and Mother Delores Blakely

INTRODUCTION

We praise you, O Lord, and thank you for the opportunity for the Lang Watson Foundation to write and publish ***"The Soul of Our Family, A Book of Prayers, Praises, and Poems ..."*** This book also includes words of blessings, meditations, and affirmations.

We are honored and humbled to share this book with family members young and old, friends and neighbors, our Christian community, and spiritually minded people throughout the World. This book introduces prayer to those who do not know the power of prayer and meditation and seeks to help them strengthen their relationships with family and GOD.

Thank you, Father, for giving us this project that has served as an instrument to strengthen our family and spiritual ties. Above all, as a family, we have made a commitment to serve you as we carry out the legacy of the Lang Watson family ancestors.Lord, we accept prayer is an essential part of our daily family life. We recognize that through prayer, You help us to move beyond ourselves because You are our highest source of wisdom, direction, knowledge, strength, and understanding.

We thank You for this project and the contributors, who through their tireless work and private conversations with You, have made this book possible.We dedicate this book to You and present and future generations who desire to strengthen their faith and personal relationships with family and God.Your humble servants,

S. Claudia Lang Pitts, President LWF, and
Lang Watson Family Members

PRAYERS

A LETTER TO BIG DADDY

Please read this to Big Daddy for me: (Reverend Claude Lang Birth Date: March 6, 1902. Transition: March 11, 2009, 5:42 a.m.)

Dear Big Daddy,

I want you to know that my family and I have been praying for you. I know you are probably weary and tired. You are surrounded by a family who loves you deeply, as I do. I can only speak for myself in saying that I just do not want to see you go. You mean everything to me and have given life to this big family, and we love you for that and all you have done for each and every one of us. It has been a long time since I have seen you in person. Big Daddy, please wait for me and other family members who have not yet made it to see you. I want you to know my family and I will be coming to see you on March 19th. Our son Brandon sends his blessings and prays for you but is unable to make it. Happy Birthday, Big Daddy, and I'll see you soon.

Love Jr. and family.

Wilbur Harris, Jr., Colorado
March 6, 2009

MY DAILY PRAYER

Lord God of the ages. Thou art worthy of all praise and glory, the world and they that dwell therein are your creation. The light and the darkness are as the same to thee. You speak to the wind, and it obeys. You command the sun and the stars to shine. You are God and God alone.

Lord God, thank you for answering prayers and for your care and love. I bless your name and thank you for 2 Corinthians 5:18-20 and all things that are of God who hath given us the ministry of reconciliation.

5:20 - Now then are we ambassadors for Christ, as though God did beseech you by us, we pray you in Christ's stead, be ye reconciled to God.

Because I am an ambassador of Christ, I pray the Lord's blessings over my family. I affirm and declare; I am God's child. - 1 Peter 1:23. I affirm and declare, I am forgiven of all my sins and washed in the blood. - Ephesians 1:7, Hebrews 9:14

I affirm and declare; I am the temple of the Holy Spirit. - 1 Corinthians 6:19

I affirm and declare; I am strong in the Lord. - Ephesians 6:10

The Lord pours out his spirit on my offspring and his blessing on my sisters, brothers, and grandchildren (all descendants) as written in Isaiah 49:25 and 26.

I (Speak Your Name) declare healing over my body. I declare healing over my spirit man. For He was wounded for our transgressions, He was bruised for our iniquities, and the chastisement of our peace was upon Him, and by His stripes we are healed. James 4:7 and 8, "therefore submit to God, resist the devil and he will flee from you. Draw near to God and He will draw near to you. Be healed, be delivered, be set free. For I am healed, delivered, and set free, in Jesus' holy and righteous name, Amen.

Say this prayer for 30 days, and your faith will be stronger than the mustard seed.

Bishop John Edward Lang, Sr.

PSALMS 29:11

Dear Diary: October 3, 1975

Read my Bible. Pray continually.

The Lord will give strength unto his people; the Lord will bless his people with peace. Psalms 29:11

Missionary Phyllis E. Y. Lang Adams

FAMILY DAILY!

Psalm 91 is a family prayer for the Flynns. May the Lord strengthen and bless all families! Jesus says: if my people that are called by my Name seek my face, ask for forgiveness of their sins, and turn from their wicked ways, then He can hear and heal the LAND!

I believe in the 3 Ps, which are Pray, Plead, then Praise!

Crystal and Juan Flynn

CRY JESUS

Oh, Saints of God, do you know how and when to cry Jesus?

In Your heart you say yes, but do we really know? There is no time or special place to call our Saviors name.

- When things look dark and cloudy, cry Jesus.
- When the sun shines bright and strong, cry Jesus.
- When the road is rugged and sometimes bent, don't fall away and lose your strength. Cry Jesus.
- When a sister or brother falls by the way, don't start to talk, pray and help them walk the holy way, and cry Jesus.
- When the pastor preaches the Word, and it cuts you to the quick, don't grumble. Move up a little higher, give the devil a good hard kick, and cry Jesus.
- When your neighbor lets the devil ride and say things that hurt deep inside, forgive them, hold your peace, and cry Jesus.
- When it's ashes to ashes and dust to dust time, give God the glory, pray for the ones that were left behind, and cry Jesus.
- Now, God has blessed you with a new home, a better car, and everything is fine. You have plenty now, and your empty pocket is now filled with money inside. Be thankful, and don't cheat God. Pay all of your tithes, and cry Jesus.

Missionary Nancy Ruth Lang Harvey Samuels

BLESS MY FAMILY PRAYER

O God, please bless our family, enlarge our coast and influence so that you will be glorified through us. Lord, keep your hands upon us and keep us from evil, so it will not bring grief to our family and loved ones. Please, Lord, keep us in your grace, that we may be able to love and respect each other and that we as a family pray for one other and others. Lord bless us with the know-how and the wisdom to keep the legacy of prayer for generation after generation. Amen

Missionary Leora Harvey Lockett

PSALMS 113:3

Dear Diary: October 4, 1975

Praying continually. Read my Bible.

From the rising of the sun unto the going down of the same the Lord's name is to be praised. Psalms 113: 3

Missionary Phyllis E. Y. Lang Adams

BEDTIME PRAYER

Thank you for Pa Pa. Thank you for Ma Ma. Thank you for Mommy. Thank you for my sister Hazel. Thank you for Cousin Inez.

Claudia Magee, age 4

A PERSONAL PRAYER

Dear Merciful God,

Hear my prayer from deep within my heart. I lift my voice and utter these words with expectant hope and fully rejoice about my anticipated answer. These are not empty words but are the best I can do. Recognize me beyond this withered face that is so tested and challenged by time. My gray and balding head is a monument to the well travel roads we together have shared.

So God, I share with you none other than the intimate and the personal things I only confide in you. I started this day with hope and a mind to accomplish the many feats and labors of potential. I found my dreams, aspirations, and even my foolishness massacred during the attempt. I have lost nothing but only gained more faith to try again. There is no failure in God!

The longevity I enjoy is but a moment in time spent with you. You have sustained the viability of my life because your love is ever-present. You are the substance for my faith, and your principles mitigate my personal excesses while encouraging my good. Allow this unworthy being to stand before you, one as holy as you, and then simply repent! I stand and plea because your grace has guided me in this way. I only hope that in this journey I went as far as I could today.

How could I doubt the legacy and life my forbearers have prepared for me? The Evil One has attempted to steal my recollections of what your hand as provided in substance, prayed out long ago through them. You have given me life and adorned my existence with the peace and dignity of daily relationship. I know that I am yours.Out of the abundance of your love I am able to unite my personal life in you, "Thy will be done." I acknowledge my past indiscretions, and arguments of selfish justification, only to continue wrestling with my personal desires of self-aggrandizement and the poor sensibility of how blessed I am. Teach me Lord to surrender self and follow your way. Help me to know the legitimate voice of your call. God, you alone moved me from chaos to creation, from controversy to alignment, from ego to selflessness, and you preserved me beyond the spiritual Alzheimer's that would incapacitate the memory of your sacred trust. "Thy Word have I hid in my heart that I might not sin against thee."

So God, make me the custodian of this body, soul, and spirit that is so precious! It was only you who caught me during my plunge and free-fall toward death. There is no present quest for financial, technological, political, social, or relational pursuit so enduring that I should cut my ties to godliness. Keep me, I pray. Keep my family and those I love. Keep us until the day of our redemption.

God, I thank you for the grace, salvation, sanctification, and glory authenticated in my life. Thank you for the love that embraced my frustration, handled my anxieties, provided faith rather than fate, and saved my life! My prayer is illustrative of your faithfulness to me. I am *short of breath, and words cannot speak adequately of what I owe to you. Though speak, I must!* Thank you, Holy Spirit, for sustaining your child and preserving the awareness that enabled my conscience righteously as a member of a family that loves God!

Bishop David Allen Hall, Public Saint

SEEKING YOU

"And ye shall seek me, and find me, when ye shall search for me with all your heart" - Jeremiah 29:13, KJV

Father, I come to you in prayer, seeking your presence in my life today and always

- To guide me and protect me from harm
- To teach me patience and forgiveness towards myself and then towards others
- To encourage me to seek you first and know that all other things I seek will fall in line, if ordained by you
- To protect me from self-inflicted harm and harm that can come from others.
- To show me your love, and that I will know what real love is, to give it freely and unconditionally, as you gave your love to me.

Father, I close my prayer honoring you, praising you, and thanking you for all that I am and hope to be because of the blessings you've given to me. Amen, Amen, and Amen!

Mona LaR'ose Barnes

EMOTIONAL HEALING

I come to you, Lord laying all the trauma, hurt, pain, and abuse I have experienced at the hands of others. I know that it was not your desire for me to experience this ugliness, and it was not Your will for me to pick up these thoughts, habits, and maladaptive behaviors to protect and shelter myself from being hurt again. I have been broken and bruised, but You, Jehovah Rapha, will heal and restore me when I call on Your name and put my full trust in You. Almighty, you take broken things and make them beautiful. You take broken things and make them whole again.

Here I am, broken and bruised, asking that You would make me beautiful and whole once again. You are the potter, and I am the clay. Shape me as you see fit. For, you take what has been spoiled, cracked, and damaged, and You reshape and refine them into a vessel that is worthy to be used by You.

Jehovah, I confess that I have been angry and upset with You for allowing me to be broken and abused because I did not understand how a good God could allow such horrible things to happen. I see now that the pain I have experienced is not because You are not good, but it is a product of a world of people that have been tainted by sin. I see the truth of your word in Romans 8:28. I believe all things work together for the good of those who believe.

Abbie Leona Tolbert, Imprfc Minister

BEDTIME PRAYER

Thank you for my bike. Thank you for giving shelters for people without homes. Thank you for giving service animals for disabled people. Protect animals.

Inez Love, age 10

GLORIFICATION AND PRAISE

For with God, nothing shall be impossible - "Luke 1:37." Peace I leave with you. My peace I give unto you. Let not your heart be troubled, neither let it be afraid – "John 14:27."

Dear Heavenly Father, I come before you with an open and humble heart to thank you and praise you for your grace and mercy. You knew of me before I was born, blessed me with living parents and siblings. Parents that worshipped, loved, and served you, Lord.

Heavenly Father, I glorify your name, Hallelujah. Thank you, Lord, for the many blessings you have bestowed upon me and my family. You have been better to me than I have been to myself. When I was in darkness, you became the light. When I was hungry, you fed me. When my soul was lost, you became my guide and restored my soul. Without God, there would be no me.Thank You! Thank You! Thank You!

Hazel Lang Mace

THANKFUL

Thank you, Heavenly Father, for loving us.
Thank you, Heavenly Father, for your patience.
Thank you for your long-suffering toward us.

Heavenly Father, help us through this Pandemic,
to stay connected with one another.
Lord, you are our helper.
Lord, you are our strength.

I am thankful you not only hear our prayers,
but you can answer our prayers.
Lord, I lift the last, the least, and the lost.

Lord, I pray that you provide peace, provision, and divine protection.

Amen.

Lisa Lampkin Magee

MY PRAYER IS...

My prayer is based on the past and for the future. The past, of my ancestral blood flowing through me who were faced with difficulties more trying than today's experiences. The future, for my posterity enduring for a much better day than our forefathers. I also pray that the ones growing up now will appreciate where they came from and strive for a better day for their offspring, and be forever blessed.

As for the matter of the current terrible world plague, we WILL get around it, over it, and through it. Remember, we've been here before. The struggle has been immense. And with the help of man's ingenuity, persistence, and God's help, we'll be fine.

Smiley Lang

BEDTIME PRAYER

Lord, I come to you today to ask for forgiveness of all my sins. Please forgive my family too. I hope that you help us through this pandemic. Bless other people with sickness or hunger. In Jesus' name I pray. Amen.

Empress Love, age 12

SELF-REJECTION

***"For if our heart condemn us, God is greater than our heart, and knoweth all things."* 1 John 3:20, KJV**

Lord, hear my prayer –
Lord, help me to love myself and others.
Heal me from the hurt and pain from my past Life.
Lord, heal me from self-rejection and the desecration of my mind, body, and spirit, and let them be a vessel to carry forth your will and plan for my life.

Lord, teach me not to seek the adoration, approval, or praise of others to inflate a false ego, but help me understand that your unconditional love and acceptance are sufficient.

And Lord, I humbly request that you strengthen me and free me from the bondage of self-rejection and help me to understand that I belong to you – 'The family of God.' Amen.

S. Claudia Lang Pitts

BEDTIME PRAYER

Now I lay me down to sleep.

I pray to the Lord my soul to keep.

If I should die, before I wake,

I pray to the Lord my soul to take.

Amen

S.D. Mitchell and G.W. Myer
Submitted by Amanda Charles

A MOTHER'S PRAYER

Mary Lang, the late mother of De Edward, Will, Smiley, and Yvonne, cousins of the late Elder Claude Lang, left her family with a legacy of Love and Biblical prayers:

Dear Children,

I pray for all of you without ceasing (1Thessalonians 5:17) and that you would build a personal relationship with God. I pray that you will also build your own prayer priorities through God's Holy Word. I will keep on being glad because I know that your prayers and the help that comes from the Spirit of Christ Jesus will keep us safe (Philippians 1:19).

For I know that my redeemer lives *(Job 19:25)! So, I will be alert. Stand firm in the faith. Be courageous. Be strong. And do everything in LOVE. (1 Corinthians 16:13.14). Remember, whatever you do, do well (Ecclesiastes 9:10). So do not get weary in well-doing, for at just the right time, you shall reap a harvest of blessings if you don't give up (Galatians 6:9). AMEN

These are some instructions I have learned from reading my Holy Bible. I trust God's word, and I pray that you will always pray for each other. Remember, love is the greatest gift you can give each other as you pray to our Heavenly Father. Pray on, my children.

*Mother Lang's favorite scripture is on her headstone as she awaits the resurrection.

Mary and De Edward Lang

PSALMS 106:1

Dear Diary: October 5, 1975

Read my Bible. Praying continually.

Praise ye the Lord. I give thanks unto the Lord, for he is good, for his mercy endureth forever.

Psalms 106:1

Missionary Phyllis E. Y. Lang Adams

HERE I KNEEL

Father, I kneel before you today, in perfect awe of your greatness. I come with words of praise on my mind and a song of gratefulness in my soul.

I come not asking for a handout or hand up. This time I just come to praise you!

You've blessed me in more ways than I can say, given me more than I could ever repay.

You've given me plenty of examples of what it's like to have GOD on your side, in my own family

Your never-ending patience toward me has taught me to have patience with my own wonderful boys.Through your mercy toward me, I've learned to have empathy for others and to count my blessings each time I start feeling low, left out, or pitying myself.

I choose to be grateful even when things aren't going the way I want them to. Because I know you make no mistakes and have a plan for me! I choose to follow your word, guidance, and example. I have no reason to follow any false profit or other spiritual beings because you have shown me that you are the one and only living GOD that reigns.

Father, I lift you up in praise. I worship you and adore you for my very being!

- For the eyes that you've given me to see the world that you created for us, your children.
- For my hands and arms to lift and shout praises to you, to wave them back in forth in praise of you, to stretch them across the left and right side of me, holding on tight to feel your love just when I need you the most.
- For my voice to sing hallelujah after hallelujah in awe of all that you've done just for me and this world that continues to forsake you when all you ask is that we love you and acknowledge you.

So, I will continue to praise you, and look to you for my strength, just because of who you are – GOD all by yourself! In the holy name of Jesus -AMEN and AMEN and AMEN!

Mona LaR'ose Lampkin Barnes

GOOD MORNING LORD

Father God:

How grateful I am for you waking me up. Not only am I so very thankful for your giving me the gift of life but for allowing me to worship and praise you for your mercy that endures forever. I have the privilege of offering back to you my life and this day to do your will, your way. I need you to cleanse me and forgive me from all my sins, known and unknown. I repent of all that has offended you and your people. Give me the right spirit, Your Holy Spirit, to obey you.

Lord, I am indebted to you for numerous reasons, and You alone can help me give you the worship that you are worthy of. "You are worthy, O Lord, to receive glory and honor and power; For You created all things, And by Your will, they exist and were created." Revelation 4:10b. You are the only God, All righteous, the Holy One, Mighty in Splendor, the Daystar. Almighty, the Captain of the Army of Hosts, My Redeemer, The One who is soon to come.

I am so grateful for the godly heritage I have been given, for grandparents who were truly saved and walked their talk. There is not a day that I cannot praise you for how spiritually rich I am.

God, because of your sacrificial death and resurrection, my godly examples come from my saved parents and relatives. I wanted what they had. I said yes to salvation early at 12 yrs. of age. You have been faithful to me down through the years when I was unfaithful to you. You kept me from any danger that I was unable to keep myself from. Your Grace has showered me with favor, way beyond whatever I was did. You have magnified yourself to me, not because I was or am good because You alone are good.

I thank you for extended life and for allowing me to know you more and more.

It is my prayer that I would live to bring You Glory every day. Amen

Dr. Joan A. (Watson) Ganns

INTERCESSORY PRAYER FOR LOVED ONES

For verily I say unto you, that whosoever shall say unto this mountain, Be thou removed, and be thou cast into the sea; and shall not doubt in his heart but shall believe that those things which he saith shall come to pass; he shall have whatsoever he saith. Mark 11:23, KJV

But if ye do not forgive, neither will your Father which is in heaven forgive your trespasses.

Mark 11:26, KJV

Father God, in Jesus' name, I pray for you to bless my son to get a kidney transplant. We trust in you and that everything will work out that he will receive a kidney. Father, thank you for blessing me and all our family. In Jesus name, Amen

Father God, please bless my friend. My granddaughter and I take care of him. He is sick with asthma and Alzheimer's. Father God, please take those illnesses away from him.

Thank you in Jesus' name, Amen.

Clara Phillips

PSALMS 144:15

Dear Diary: October 25, 1975

Read my Bible. Praying continually.

Happy is that people that is in such a case: yea, happy is that people, whose God is the Lord.

Psalms 144:15

Missionary Phyllis E. Y. Lang Adams

MY STRENGTH

"Lord grant me the serenity to accept the things I cannot change, courage to change the things I can, and wisdom to know the difference."

As I sit and reflect on my life while we are in these unprecedented times of 2020, I smile with warmth in my heart with a deep appreciation for my family for providing me with the opportunity to achieve success and thrive in my own American Dream. When I was ever doubtful of my ability to be a positive light in this world, I never folded because of my family's strong support and the constant reminder that our bloodline is legendarily strong. I am immensely proud of who we are and honestly believe that with our strong faith and ability to overcome that, we will be ok throughout these changing times because nothing is strong enough to change our love.

Lawrence G. Lampkin

GOD OF THE UNIVERSE, EARTH, HEAVENS, AND ALL MEN

We ask for your forgiveness and to grant us strength in our spirit. We ask you to protect those who know your name and to guide anyone still seeking you.

We reach out to you in sincerity and humbleness to help guide us through these tumultuous times.

To soften our hearts and tongues and to strengthen our minds to endure any dark times ahead.

We beg you to forgive humanity, as we are mere children still growing from past experiences, abuse, poverty, entitlements, and narcissism.

Though in these times, it is hard to have faith in one another, please continue to build bridges between people of diverse backgrounds but the same moral integrity.

Thank you for sending living angels to provide knowledge, morality, and leadership. Although their time on earth seemed short, it was fulfilled and inspired generations.

Bless and strengthen anyone who has lost loved ones and cover those who have lost livelihoods.

We thank you for knowing we are flawed and loving us despite our flaws.

We thank you for each day of breath and new beginnings.

We thank you for our beautiful home on earth and hope to live in your likeness so that we will make it to our spiritual home in heaven.

Amen.

Claudia M. Owens

PRAYER OF PRAISE

Father God, you are so faithful. You are merciful. You are Full of Grace and Truth.You are high and lifted. We honor you.

We thank you for another chance to approach your throne to obtain mercy today.

We seek you today. We seek after you today.We give you glory for all the things you have done for us.

Thank you for breath in our bodies. Thank you for your protection.

We bless you. God, we seek your face today.

As the deer seeks after the water, so does my soul seek after you.

Today I bring my thoughts into submission to your will.

You have given us power and authority.You have given us a right to declare your word over our lives as children of the Most-High.

We thank you for your strength today. Even though sometimes we don't feel it, we know that you are still working on our behalf.

God, today we ask that as we decrease, we pray that you would increase in us.

We ask that you stir us up in our spirits today.

Father, let your word stand up in us.

We ask that you come into our hearts.

Fill every room in our hearts. Fill every space in our minds.

Holy Spirit, consume us and take over.

Sometimes we don't know what to pray for God. We pray that you would help us.

God, lead us and guide us. Your word is a lamp unto our feet and a light unto our path.

We know that you won't lead us astray, for you are always with us.

You are our Shepherd. God, transform us by your word. For your word is life.

You are the bread of life. Your word is alive and active. God work through us today. We trust you. We believe what you have said about us.

So, settle our hearts. Settle our minds. I speak peace in the mind.Your word says, "for he will keep you in perfect peace whose mind is stayed on him."

Father, you are merciful, and we ask that you forgive us.

Forgive us of any thoughts that are not like you.

Forgive us for any negative thoughts that we think about ourselves or our future.

God help our unbelief. Build our faith today.

We receive your word by faith. Amen

Fredalyn Lang

INTERCESSORY PRAYER FOR MY FRIEND

Dear Lord,

I call on behalf of my sister and dearest friend, who, if able, would lift her voice to Heaven and request healing for her precious body, the vessel that carries your gift of life.

Lord, whatever illness is harboring itself within her body, we ask in your name that it be eradicated. Immerse her in love and peace.

Even though my friend has lived alone for many years, she was not alone, for we know you have been with her every step of the way. Through educational pursuits, years of parenting, work pursuits and career successes, periods of loneliness, and when financial stresses mounted then subsided, you were there. When she suffered the loss of a loved one, you were always there to bring comfort. Whenever her humanitarian spirit led her to perform acts of kindness for family and friends – you were there cheering her on.Lord, the Coronavirus pandemic crisis prevents us, her loved ones, from being with her at this time of her deadly affliction. But we know you are there.

Until we, her family and friends can be with her again, we leave her in your care on this day of our Lord, October 29, 2020, Amen.

S. Claudia Lang Pitts

COVID FREE

Father, I come to you with a special prayer for my family for this very uncertain time due to COVID and the blood of injustice shed by Blacks all over this country for no reason, yet again.

I ask for you to cover my children with the blood of the lamb,

to protect them from COVID and injustice, harm, and hate.

I ask that you protect my family from the destruction and death that Satan brings with this disease and hate used to destroy and kill all in Satan's path.

Father help my family to stay alert and not take down their guard. Give them the insight and information that they need to understand the power of the disease and what precautions they need to continue to exercise to protect our entire family so we can be together again. Help them understand the power of hate and give them wisdom to react in a way that will protect them from harm.

Father, help us to understand how blessed we are not to have lost many loved ones in 2020. Give us the strength to get through the days without those loved ones that have gone home to meet with you. Thank you for allowing them to be a part of our lives and us a part of theirs for as long as we have had them. Help us to understand that we are all here for a moment, that this world is just a stop along the way, that hate is a poison developed by man, and love is more powerful because it comes from you and will always win.

Help us to be encouraged in knowing that we shall see those that have gone before us, again in heaven but next time forever!

Father, keep the Lang – Watson Family in your arms of protection forever and ever In Jesus' holy name – Amen and Amen and Amen!

Mona LaR'ose Lampkin Barnes

IN YOUR NAME

"The Lord is my rock, and my fortress, and my deliverer, my God, my strength, in whom I will trust; my buckler, and the horn of my salvation, and my high tower." Psalm 18:1, KJV

I am STABLE and STRONG. I am STRONG and COURAGEOUS.

"Have not I commanded thee? Be strong and of a good courage; be not afraid, neither be thou dismayed: for the LORD, thy God is with thee whithersoever thou goest." Joshua 1:9, KJV

God, we ask that you protect us from opinions and ideas that the enemy has tried to make us believe and sway us from your word.We ask that you lift the burden of anxiety. We bind anxiety in Jesus' name.

We rebuke the spirit of scattered thoughts. We rebuke and denounce the spirit of fear.

We rebuke negative thoughts about ourselves and our future. We rebuke thoughts of uncertainty.

We cast our burdens on you, God. You are all-knowing, all-powerful, and always present with us.

You can handle it, so we give them you, even the hidden things God.

The places that only you know about.

We bind the spirit of exhaustion. God, we are tired in our minds. We pray against burnout.

We pray against being overwhelmed in our spirits, feeling overworked.

But we won't faint. We won't stop. We won't give up.

God build us up where we are weak, for you said that your strength is made perfect in our weakness.

So, God, I command my mind to be healed. I command my mind to be delivered.

I command my mind to be set free.We submit to your authority.

Deliver us from all unrighteousness. Deliver us from anything that is not like you.

Cleanse us. Wash us. Purge us. Purify us. Purify our thoughts. Purify our intentions.

This we ask in your name. Amen.

Fredalyn Lang

FORGIVENESS AND PRAISE

Dear Father God, first, I would like to ask for your forgiveness for all my sins, committed and omitted - knowingly and unknowingly. I immediately thank you for forgiveness. Lord, I humbly bow before you to give you all the Praise, all the Honor, and for all your Glory. It belongs to you alone.

You are so magnificent and so marvelous in all your ways. I thank you today and for the rest of my days. As a result of your illustrious shine, I can pray and know that you will surely answer in your own time. You have allowed me to be free, and I will forever be grateful to thee.

I thank the Lord, for his truth is protection, like his shield and sword. His affection is perfection. His attention is the longest and strongest. His love is everywhere and evident to share. That is why I offer this prayer. Just to show your love, pay continual thanks, homage, remembering, reminiscing, thinking, and thanking you for all you've done, are doing, and will do. Consequently, keeping me and mine above. In Jesus' mighty name. Amen, amen and amen.

Marietta L. Hall

JAMES 3:17-18

Dear Diary: December 24, 1975

Read my Bible. Praying continually.

But in His wisdom that is from above is first pure, then peaceable, gentle, and easy to be interested, full of mercy and good fruits, without partiality, and without hypocrisy and the fruit of righteousness is sown in peace of them that make peace.

James 3:17-18

Missionary Phyllis E. Y. Lang Adams

GOD'S HEART

The Natural Man

The Natural Man has no understanding of God due to no Holy Spirit. This is the reason some of our family members cannot stand being around us.

The Mind of Christ

Having the mind of God is living daily by His word. It is through our having the Holy Ghost in our heart we can begin to know the thoughts of God. We do this by spending time with Him, fasting, and praying. Along with this, we consistently stay in the words of God.

We should look for an opportunity and be ready to serve His people. This serving should come from the heart of His saints. Are you able to lay aside your rights, even opportunities, to be enabled to serve others? This is having a Christ-like mind. The mind of Christ requires our thinking and doing as He would think daily. Yes, considering others before ourselves. In essence, this gives us spiritual insight, using the attributes of the fathers due to the spirit being our heart.

The Carnal Man

Where are you in your spiritual growth cycle? Are you an infant, or are you an adolescent, or are you an adult saint? Check this out. If you have been quarreling like children, allowing divisions or differences of opinion to draw your attention. That is another place where we are feeding the carnal man and not being like Christ. Continue to check yourself to know you are not driving for a position that God does not want you to have.

The Spiritual Man

Know the history of the Holy Spirit. You know God is three persons in one. God the Father, God the Son, and God the Holy Spirit. God became a man in Christ Jesus so that He could die for our sins. Jesus Christ rose from the dead to offer salvation to all through rebirth and spiritual renewal. Jesus left this great world we know, but He said He would pray to the father to send a comforter. That he did, and it is here right now as a keeper for the spiritual man, in our everyday life. This gives us the presence of God 24/7 until Jesus comes back again. Before Jesus Christ came to earth, the Holy Spirit empowered specific believers for specific purposes for God. Now we all believe and know God has the power. It is available to us at all times. Believing is both trusting what the word of God says and relying on it daily. It is believing He will give us the power to change our lives. He lets us know in His Word that saints may have momentarily doubt, but they never reject God. Unbelievers are those that reject or ignore God completely. They have a sinners 'heart!

Pastor Milton L. Hall Jr.

THOUGHTS OF PEACE

"For I know the thoughts that I think toward you, saith the Lord, thoughts of peace, and not of evil, to give you an expected end. Jeremiah 29:11, KJV

I command my mind to think thoughts of peace.

We loose healing today. We loose the joy of the Lord today. We loose strength today.

We loose freedom today. We loose victory in the mind.

Pull down every stronghold that is keeping us from seeking you the more.

Remove every hindrance that is trying to keep us from breaking through.

Pull down every stronghold hold that takes away our desire to read the Bible.

Remove every distraction that is trying to keep us from worshipping you.

Remove whatever is keeping us busy and preventing us from praying to you. You are our priority.

Thank you, Father. We surrender. We repent, Father. We appreciate you.We acknowledge you as Lord of our life. We love you. We adore you.We worship you. We magnify you. We bless you.

Thank you because all things are well concerning us.

In Jesus' name. Amen.

By Fredalyn Lang

MY GOD, THANK YOU

The God Who hovers and moves over the face of the earth and His beloved children who inhabit it is the magnificent Creator of the heavens and the earth. You see the goodness in things, approve them and say so. Thank you for all the blessed goodness you bestow on us all, the sunshine and the rain, fruits and plants, wildlife and family. Thank you for Your provision and generosity.

Thank You for blessing the seventh day, our day of Sabbath rest in You. It is holy and set apart just as You are. You are set apart on high and yet close enough for us to touch the hem of Your garment and be healed; to rest upon Your chest and know Your love; to be shielded from so much more than we know under the shadow of your wings; to be led to still waters and green pastures where You assure us every time ... You are God.

Thank You for the grace and mercy in our lives renewed every day. We need it. Thank you also for walking in fellowship with us and putting that same desire in our hearts. You go before us, make crooked places straight, never leave us nor forsake us, and let us know that the battle is not ours, but Yours and is already won. Thank You also for covering us in our nakedness and sending your Word to deliver us from our destructions. Thank you for forgiving me and teaching me to forgive as You do.

I pray for the ability to honor You with obedience to your ways and your Word and plan for my life. Help me trust beyond my understanding of things I see and experience, knowing you hold me in the palm of Your hand and have plans to prosper me and give me hope and a future. I pray I use my words wisely, therefore keep watch over my mouth, and keep the gate of my lips. Your Words of instruction and correction, and all I need is a masterful example of how to do things simply wonderfully, with love as inspiration and joy, peace, humility, gentleness, long-suffering, faith, and goodness inspiring my steps. Thank You, my Jehovah Eli.

Ruth Lang

SEEKING YOU AND THANKING YOU GOD

Dear Heavenly Father, please hear my prayer.

I pray that you help me to help my family.

Please mold me and use me to bring you glory, Father.

I pray today for forgiveness.

I pray for understanding of circumstances that are under your control.

I pray that I'm able to bless those you would have me to bless.

I pray for your continued covering of our family.I know my strength is only because of you.

Father, I thank you for all the grace and mercy you always show to our family.

In the name of Jesus – Amen

Curtis J. Pound

A FAMILY PRAYER

LORD, thank you for the love you give and the caring that you show. Thank you for the words and wisdom that keep us close to you even when we don't deserve it. LORD, continue to watch over us and keep us safe from all the harm and dangers of this cruel and unjust world. LORD, you are great and all-powerful, and your love is forever lasting. Amen.

Mark R. Harvey

SUBMIT TO GUIDANCE

Dear Heavenly Father,

I pray today for Guidance through difficult circumstances.

You know the kind of situations where you can't navigate out of without spiritual guidance.I need you to strengthen me so that my mind doesn't get weary in practicing your will, Lord.

I need guidance from you, Lord, so I know that small voice from you is providing me with explicit direction in your will. Father, I pray that you guide me in such a way that my light will get brighter and my mind's focus gets sharper.

Guide me, Lord, in love, in forgiveness, in health, in gratefulness, in appreciation, in finance, in family. I need to hear a word of guidance daily to move in the right direction.

In Jesus Name – Amen

Curtis J. Pounds

IT'S UP TO ME

I treat myself with genuine self-respect and compassion every day. I tell the negative voice in my head to go somewhere else and only make space for loving, compassionate self-talk.

I prioritize my health and think about what is truly serving me with each decision I make to take care of my body.

I know exactly what needs to get done today to grow my career and myself, and I am committed to getting it done in a productive and efficient way.

I forgive myself for being imperfect because I am human. Every perceived failure provides an opportunity to learn and grow.

I am kind, compassionate, and genuine to others. Listening and holding space for them is a powerful gift.

I feel amazed when I wake up early, dedicate a few moments to myself, and move my body. I am committed to this habit and proud of myself for upholding it.

I continuously remind myself to be present. Maximizing the now is more important than dwelling on the past or fretting over the future.

I prioritize drinking more water and taking my vitamins daily.

My goals are valid, and I am fully equipped to achieve them. I believe in myself and take the necessary steps every day to fulfill my dreams of having a successful career, quality family time, and positive social life.

I am enough. Right now. Just the way I am.

Lawrence G. Lampkin

WATCH OVER US

Lord, Jesus, watch over my family, my friends, and more. Give me strength, confidence, and hope, Lord Jesus, when I feel alone. Guide me on the right path in school and the choices I make out of school. Watch over those who are in hard times. May the virus pass over, and they find a cure, Lord Jesus. Amen

Love Barnes.

FAITHFULNESS

"Because of the Lord's great love, we are not consumed. For his compassions never fail. They are new every morning. Great is your faithfulness." Lamentations 3:22-23

My prayer is to continue to thank my Lord, God, and Savior for the privilege of beginning each and every day by talking to him. I give you myself and my schedule asking to be used to further your Kingdom. Grant me the wisdom to handle each situation I encounter with grace so that my speech will be pleasing and my thoughts pure as I follow your directions.

I am so incredibly grateful that the plans you have for me are good, and I trust in your steadfast faithfulness. Help me to live in a manner worthy of the calling you have placed on my life and to magnify your name in all things. The Lord's loving-kindness indeed never ceases. "They are new every morning. Great is your faithfulness." Amen

Patricia Ann Charles Harvey

PRAYER FOR COVERING

The blood of the living Christ be applied to all the children of God. The blood covers and solidifies our faith. The blood of the lamb of God shall never lose its power to cleanse, save, protect, purge, and deliver his saints.

Bishop John E. Lang, Sr.

GRATEFUL

Father, God, thank you for this day. You are my everything! I submit my mind, my heart, my soul, and my strength to you today. Lord, thank you for allowing me to awaken to see this day. A day that is brand new with a fresh and renewed spirit.

Father, God, align my mind and my spirit Lord, so that I may see and hear what I must do for you and your people. Jesus, hold my hand. Help me see what you see in me. I love you, Jesus, because of who you are. Thank you, Jesus, for protection. Thank you for waving to me. Thank you, Lord, for all the abundant blessings that you have bestowed on our Lang / Watson Family. When I think about all the times you showed up and showed out, all I can say is,

THANK YOU, LORD.

THANK YOU, JESUS.

YOU KEEP ON BLESSING OUR FAMILY!

Curtis J. Pounds

MIRACLES, SIGNS, AND WONDERS

"But was wounded for our transgressions, he was bruised for our iniquities: the chastisement of our peace was upon him; and with his stripes we are healed." Isaiah 53.5, KJV

Evangelist De Ella White Hall

PRAYERS TO OUR FATHER IN JESUS' NAME

"Follow peace with all men, and holiness, without which no man shall see the Lord:" Hebrews 12:14

We come to you as humble and reverent children seeking your abundant grace and mercy. We realize and honor your sovereign, divine power. Please lift us up when we have fallen. Lead us in your righteousness. Enable us to faithfully discharge our divine purpose with joy. If we cause any hurt or injury to our fellow man, please forgive and restore us in love. We seek to be a blessing in all our relationships, spiritual and secular. We receive your word for our daily instruction. Hebrews 12:14 to follow peace with all men. Bless us with your divine favor, all in Jesus' name.

Bishop John E. Lang Sr.

YOUR PERSONAL PRAYER OF FORGIVENESS

Heavenly Father, I come to you in Jesus Christ's holy name. I thank you for being omnipotent. I praise you for being omniscient. I praise you for your sovereignty and righteousness. I thank you for answering prayers. I thank you for hearing my cry. I humbly submit my spirit, soul, and body to be the temple of your holy spirit. Lord, I have a problem with forgiveness. Teach me to forgive. I know your word in Ephesians 1:6-7 "To the praise of the glory of his grace wherein he hath made us accepted in the beloved. In whom we have redemption thru his blood, the forgiveness of sins, according to the riches of his grace."

You have forgiven my sins and washed them away in your righteous blood. I thank you and bless your name. I (Speak Your Name) ask that you change my heart so that I might forgive. For your word in Matthew 6:14-15 says, "For if ye forgive men their trespasses, your heavenly Father will also forgive you. Matthew 15 says, "But if ye forgive not men their trespasses, neither will your Father forgive your trespasses."

Lord, I understand when I receive your command to forgive, cast out the vengeful spirit, change me just as 2 Corinthians 5:17 says. "Therefore if any man be in Christ, he is a new creature; old things are passed away; behold all things are become new." in Jeremiah 29:11, it says, "For I know the thoughts that I think toward you, saith the Lord, thoughts of peace, and not of evil, to give you an expected end." To err is human. To forgive is divine. From this day forward, I (Speak Your Name) commit my will to be in subjection to your will. To forgive those that have harmed me, those that have spoken evil of me, those that have betrayed me, those that have lied on me, those that have physically abused me. Lord help me to cast it with you into the sea of forgetfulness. I (Speak Your Name) do affirm, declare, decree, by your righteousness so help me God, In the name of our Lord Jesus Christ.

Bishop John E. Lang, Sr.

THANK YOU

Thank you God for keeping us safe and thank you for the Earth.

Talia Iris Weiss, age 6

MY PERSONAL RELATIONSHIP WITH GOD

"And we know that all things work together for good, to them that love God to them who are called according to his purpose." Romans 8:28

Lord, reveal your purpose for my life and help me to walk in the path that you have prepared for me. Shield me from the ungodly ways of the World and protect me from the evildoers. Lord, encourage my heart and strengthen my faith as I await word from You. I know that You are in 'absolute control' and working on my behalf, removing every obstacle that can hinder me from fulfilling your purpose.Lord, when I am weak, help me to see that 'self-life' desires within me may cause me to act independently of your will. Help me to distinguish the desires of the flesh from those human desires that are aligned with the Holy Spirit.Lord, I desire my personal relationship with You to grow stronger each day so that when I fall on my knees to have uninterrupted prayer with You, I am able to be a better listener and learn -- when you speak to me. Thank You for being the source of my love and strength, and thank you for the blessings You bestow upon me and my loved ones every day. Amen.

S. Claudia Lang Pitts

LOVE ONE ANOTHER

Let us forgive one another and love as God has commanded, "This is my commandment, That ye love one another, as I have loved you."I thank you, heavenly Father, for family and friends and those who read this prayer. I pray your peace in the midst of a troubled world. Bless our families to love and honor each other. Lord, I thank you for our inheritance given among those that are sanctified given to us through our parents and grandparents. They left a legacy of holiness and righteous living and a life of prayer. I thank you for the families that are connected by blood and by your spirit. My prayer if you don't know Jesus Christ as your Savior is that you accept Him today. God Bless you.

Evangelist DeElla White Hall

A BLESSING AND PRAYERS OF THE RIGHTEOUS

Lord God, we come to you. Lord God, we thank you and bless your name. Lord God, we come to you as humble and meek children. We pray glory and honor to your holy and righteous name. Therefore, we cry Abba, Father God. We lift our hands in submission without wrath or doubting. Hallowed be your holy and mighty name. Father, hear and act on the prayers of your children. We thank you for the salvation of our souls. Therefore we pray John 3:16. We ask for mercy and healing of our home relationships in these trying times. We ask of thee physical healing and wholeness, understanding, and wisdom. Bless our homes, our jobs, our community, our nation, and the nations of the world. Intervene, dear God. Turn around what the enemy has planned for us. Give us your amazing grace. Stretch out your hand and touch us with a loving touch.

2 Chronicles 7:14 - "If my people which are called by my name, shall humble themselves, and pray, and seek my face, and turn from their wicked ways; then will I hear from heaven, and will forgive their sin, and will heal their land." It is our desire that every believer would humble themselves before God during these trying times. Amen.

By Bishop John E. Lang, Sr.

AFFIRMATIONS OF PRAYER OVER OUR CHILDREN AND GRANDCHILDREN

"'And all thy children shall be taught of the LORD; and great be the peace of thy children." Isaiah 54:13

"For he hath made him to be sin for us, who knew no sin; that we might be made the righteousness of God in him." 2 Corinthians 5:21, KJV

"And the Lord shall make thee the head, and not the tail; and thou shalt be above only, and thou shalt not be beneath; if that thou hearken unto the commandments of the Lord thy God, which I command thee this day, to observe and to do them:" Deuteronomy 28:13, KJV.

"Being confident of this very thing, that he which hath begun a good work in you will perform it until the day of Jesus Christ:" Philippians 1:6, KJV.

Heavenly Father, in the name of your dearly beloved son Jesus Christ, I thank you and praise you for the promises in your word concerning my children and grandchildren. I affirm that all my children and grandchildren shall be taught of the Lord, and great shall be the peace of my children and grandchildren according to Isaiah 54:13.

I affirm and declare your divine protection over my children and grandchildren as they travel to and from school, college, work, or wherever they go. Thank you, dear Father, for saving them from this untoward generation.

According to your word in 2 Corinthians 5:21, my children and grandchildren are the righteousness of God in him, and they are the head and not the tail as promised in Deuteronomy 28:13. He who began a good work in my children and grandchildren will continue it until the days of Jesus Christ as found in Philippians 1:6.

By Bishop John E. Lang Sr.

COMFORT AND PEACE

"Blessed be God, even the Father of our Lord Jesus Christ, the Father of mercies, and the God of all comfort; Who comforteth us in all our tribulation, that we may be able to comfort them which are in any trouble, by the comfort wherewith we ourselves are comforted of God."

Father, though these are days of tribulations and the onset of darkness we have never seen, we as a family and a people of Your Kingdom are yet comforted!

Lord, we take comfort in Your comfort! We trust in all Your Word that says in Jeremiah 32:38

"And they shall be my people, and I will be their God:"

Only You can provide the most excellent peace Lord God! The peace you give us is excellent because it has the power to keep us! Your peace keeps our hearts and our minds in you!

Without you, we can do nothing! You are the vine, and we are the branches! From You, all life, health, strength, and blessings flow!

Let us forever and always be reminded that You want more than just us, Lord. You call all people to repentance! Your word says, "Whosoever will call upon the name of the Lord shall be saved!"

Help us, Lord, to comfort the whosoevers of this world that they may be comforted by Your comfort in us! Help us, Lord, to overcome the trouble of this world like You have overcome the world with faith, hope, and love!

Now Father be glorified by our alignment and uniting to be one church, one faith serving one God and Father of our one and only savior, the Lord Jesus Christ.

It is in Your Holy Name we pray!

Amen!

Elder Claude Lang

ALL THINGS WONDERFUL

I pray for flowers, for our family and for rainbows.

Chani Ivy Weiss, age 4

PRAYER FROM THE HEART

I pray we have more love in our hearts to unite us than fear to divide us. I pray God guides our footsteps so that we may live with purpose and promise.

I pray we honor those that have come before us by teaching their lessons to those who will be here after us.

May we live life to the fullest and show reverence for all the beauty that it holds.

Elizabeth Hazel Magee Weiss

OUR SPECIAL BIBLE PASSAGE

" 24 Now unto him that is able to keep you from falling, and to present you faultless before the presence of his glory with exceeding joy, 25To the only wise God our Savior be glory and majesty, dominion and power, both now and ever." Amen.

Jude 24-25, KJV

Al and Carla Gregory

FAITH THROUGH PRAYER

Thank you, Almighty God, for blessing me to receive my Master's Degree! It would not have been possible without your great provision and protection. I spent many days and nights studying for exams and writing papers. I found you to be faithful to show me what to study and what to write.

You gave me teachers and a fellow cohort who helped me prepare for the greatest exam of my life. When I took the exam, I had such a peace and calm, so that it was easy for me to take the exam. Thank you for the support that you gave me through my family and church.

God, I know you are real and that you are faithful to provide for my every need. Thank you that you kept me in my right mind. Thank you that you healed me and gave me health. Thank you that you enabled me, in spite of being so busy at times, to still honor you and worship you by attending my home church while going to school. You encouraged me and admonished me that going to church on a regular basis was essential for my success.

It has been worth the journey because this was your will for my life. I have found joy and fulfillment in obtaining my Master's degree. I pray for all who will also be led of the Lord to pursue their education. I pray that they would put you first and seek your face in all that they do. I pray that they would remember that it is essential to be faithful to God and keep his commands. I know that if you did it once for me, you will do it again. I thank you for helping me obtain my Doctoral degree. I pray this in Jesus' name. Amen.

Shawnette Lang

ROMANS 10:12, KJV

Dear Diary: February 1, 2001

Read my Bible. Praying continually.

There hath no temptation taken but such as is common to man. But God is faithful, who will not suffer you to be tempted above that ye are able; but will with the temptation also make a way of escape, that ye may be able to bear it. Romans 10: 13

Wherefore let him that thinketh he standeth take heed lest he fall.

Romans 10:12, KJV

Missionary Phyllis E. Y. Lang Adams

MY PRAYER TO GOD

God, we thank you for the many blessings that you have bestowed upon us. Thank you for each day of life that you have blessed us to see. Oh, may we not take for granted your goodness toward us. Be merciful unto us and bless us, and cause thy face to shine upon us.

Lord, forgive me, cover my home, my children (if any), and all of my relatives and friends. Please Lord, grant that my heart be drawn closer to you that I may assure a relationship of servanthood to worship you, as my God and Father, and Jesus Christ, thy Son, who gave his life to save me from my sins, thereby reconciling me with God, the maker of heaven and earth. I learn that according to John 6:44, *"No one can come to Jesus unless the Father who sent him draws them, and Jesus will raise them up at the last day."* Draw me nearer to thee, blessed Lord; cast me not away, allow me to be thy child, and let me have a closer walk with thee. Show me the path that I must use, and I shall walk therein. I will yield myself to thy teaching and will obey thy instructions.

Protect us from diseases, including the Coronavirus Disease pandemic. REBUKE DEATH! Strengthen the weak. Rejoice the hearts of those that are oppressed. Heal other sicknesses as well. Reclaim the backslider. Lift up the saints. Comfort those that mourn. Rescue those that are in trouble. Deliver those that are bound. Remember the petitions, which are before you. Help the needy, and give a miracle to the person that prays this prayer. In Jesus' name. Amen.

Love in Jesus,

Pastor Emmanuel John

THANK YOU, JESUS

Dear Jesus, Son of the True and living God, I just lift my heart and bow my spirit to say thank you. I have come this far by faith in You. Thank You for my family, friends, and even my foes. Your love is real and has delivered me to this day. Bless me, God, this day to be a blessing to someone. I want You, Lord, to touch someone's life today. With a grateful heart, I bless you for hearing and honoring this prayer. In Jesus Name. Amen.

Craig Harvey

MY PRAYER TO GOD FOR YOU

Psalm 20

1. The Lord hear thee in the day of trouble; the name of the God of Jacob defends thee;
2. Send thee help from the sanctuary, and strengthen thee out of Zion; Remember all thy offerings and accept thy burnt sacrifice; Selah.
3. Grant thee according to thine own heart and fulfil all thy counsel.
4. We will rejoice in thy salvation, and in the name of our God we will set up our banners: The Lord fulfill all thy petitions.
5. Now know I that the Lord saveth his anointed; he will hear him from his holy heaven with the saving strength of his right hand.
6. Some trust in chariots, and some in horses: but we will remember the name of the Lord our God.
7. They are brought down and fallen but we are risen and stand upright.
8. Save, Lord: let the king hear us when we call.

And…

3 John 2, Beloved, I wish above all things that thou mayest prosper and be in health, even as thy soul prospereth.

In Jesus' name. Amen.

KJV

Love you all,

First Lady, Missionary Theresa Harvey John

POEMS

MY REQUEST

For all the people to know and all the people to see,
Make me better!
For all the people to joy and for all the people to believe,
Make me better!
For all the people to have faith and for their destiny,
Make me better!
For all the people to be healed and for all the people who grieve,
Make me better!
For all the people to have hope and for all the people being freed,
Make me better!
If I am all you got and because of me the people will trust and believe,
Make me better!
This is my prayer, in fact my sustaining hope and what I need to be,
Made better!
Lord God, it is certainly up to me to receive the grace provided,
And I shall be better!

Bishop David Allen Hall, Sr

YOU KNOW ME JESUS

There were times I thought I was on point with issues.

Had all the information I could gather in the wrong places.

There were times when I got with others and
we all agreed on what I thought was right.

I could show up just about anywhere
and bring energy into the space.

Looking back, I realize that you were there the
whole time, watching over me giving me

Opportunity to recognize.

You know me Jesus!

Curtis J. Pounds

GOD'S PLAN

God's Plan was to work us to the brim when we've had enough.

God's plan was to put us through life the hardest as it is then reward us.

God's plan was to build up strong people like you, and then give you a life of luxury.

But only if all that work you've been through was to be with Him.

Kimberly Kimble and
Zori Kimble

THE PEACE OF YOUR BEST SELF

The peace of your best self,

The love of your best self,

The love of your best of life is what needs to be found.

The world smothers our creativity and inspiration,

but where we find these tools the world could never touch.

The Heart is free from the decaying
touch of this wounded world.

Find your best self through the work of your heart.

Find your best life through the work of your heart.

Live your best life through the work of your heart.

Missionary Leora Harvey Lockett

GOD'S ANGELS

Separated by flesh.

Bonded by spirit.

You are never far away.

Memories of us together are etched in my
mind, in my heart, you will always be.

God's loving Angels watching over me

Gretta Gregory

MY GRATITUDE TO YOU

Through the ups and downs and the stress and strife,
and all the difficult
times in my life.
For the "Angels of Protection,"
you've encamped
around me,
To protect me from the things
I could not see.
LORD you've always been there
to see me through, I just want to say LORD, I LOVE YOU!!!
You mean more to me than riches or
wealth, more valuable to me
than life itself.
For all the things
you've done for me, sending me
BLESSINGS unexpected and abundantly.
For all the things you've brought me through,
LORD I give my gratitude to you!!!

Juanice Petty

PRAY GOD IS LISTENING

Prayer is a conversation with God.

Talk to God like you are talking to your friend or a neighbor.

Tell God about all your troubles.

Talk to him about your goals, pain, and

Tell him that you love him.

Remember God is listening.

Pray for the healing of this land and
the people that is upon it.

God is listening.

Pray for your loved ones so that they may seek
God's glory and that they come close to him.

God is listening.

He hears your prayers day and night.

He is listening.

Have your conversation with God, he loves us, and

He is truly listening.

Missionary Leora Harvey Lockett

ROOTS OF THE LANGS

The road will go on and as the trunk of the tree,
it will have holes and tree knots for which one can grab.
and pull thine self-up to the next branch.
Some branches are weak, but they connect
to the strong trunk of the tree and
Run Deep, and Deeper with Love.
We tell our children of how we became,
Our Roots Runs Deep across the globe, near and far.
Not touched by frost but by love.
Streaming memories to the mind of yesteryears
bringing forth the roots of our Ancestors
William, Clement, Smiley, Frederick, Claude, and Hoston.
We are their results we carry them in our flesh.
Memories of keepsakes passed down by our ancestors.
As they watch from the balconies of heaven
the Roots of the Langs' are not touched by frost but by Love.
Our Roots Runs Deep.

Rose Marie Lang-Everson

SCRIPTURES TO LIVE BY FROM MY MOTHER

Thou art my hiding place; thou shalt preserve me from trouble; thou shalt compass me about with songs of deliverance. Selah. Psalm 32:7, KJV

And he said unto me, My grace is sufficient for thee: for my strength is made perfect in weakness. Most gladly therefore will I rather glory in my infirmities, that the power of Christ make rest upon me.

2 Corinthians 12:9, KJV

Debra Harvey Williams Lanham

FOR ALL THE NEGATIVES THINGS, GOD'S POSITIVE ANSWERS

You say: "its's impossible."
God says: All things are possible. (Luke 18:27)

You say: "I'm tired."
God says: I will give you rest. (Matthew 11:28-30)

You say: "Nobody really loves me."
God says: "I love you. (John 3:16 & John 13:34)

You say: "I can't go on."
God says: My grace is sufficient. (II
Corinthians 12:9 & Psalm 91:15)

You say: "I can't figure things out."
God says: I will direct your steps. (Proverbs 3:5-6)

You say: I can't do it."
God says: You can do all things. (Philippians 4:13)

You say: "I'm not able."
God says: I am able. (II Corinthians 9:8)

You say: "It's not worth it."
God says: It will be worth it. (Roman 8:28)

You say: "I can't forgive myself."
God says: I FORGIVE you. (I John 1:9 & Romans 8:1)

You say: "I can't manage."
God says: I will supply all your needs (Philippians 4:19)

You say: "I'm afraid."
God says: I have not given you a spirit of fear. (II Timothy 1:7)

You say: "I'm always worried and frustrated."
God says: Cast all your cares on ME. (I Peter 5:7)

You say: "I don't have enough faith."
God says: I've given everyone a measure
of faith. (Romans 12:3)

You say: "I'm not smart enough."
God says: I give you wisdom. (1 Corinthians 1:30)

You say: "I feel all alone."
God says: I will l never leave you or
forsake you. (Hebrews 13:5)

**Submitted by Joyce Hall Rice on behalf of
Mother Julia Ruth Watson Hall**

THE SAVIOR'S WORDS

If you never felt pain,

How would you know that I'm a healer?

If you never went through bondage,

How would you know that I am a deliverer?

If you never had a trial,

How could you call yourself an overcomer?
If you never felt sadness,
How would you know that I am a comforter?
If you never made a mistake,
How would you know that I am forgiving?
If you never were in trouble,
How would you know that I will come to your rescue?
If you never were broken,
Then how would you know that I can make you whole?
If you never had problems,
How would you know that I can solve them?
If you never had any suffering,
How would you know that I went through?
If you never went through the fire,
How would you become pure?
If I simply gave you all things,
How would you appreciate then?
If I never corrected you,
How would you know that I love you?
If you had all power,
How would you learn to depend on Me?
If your life was perfect,
What would you need Me for?

Submitted by Joyce Hall Rice on behalf of
Mother Julia Ruth Watson Hall

THE PERSON WHO WOULD BE MY GOD!

Do I need your approval?
Do I need your trust?
Do I need your respect?
Unless, I surrender you have no hope without me?
I got it now.
I truly conceived.
I confirm my belief!
Is it that, you have no joy without me?
Abnegation is a life's decision.
This is a relationship though one sided!
This is love unrequited!
Is our speech clarion and we said what we mean?
Is this a point of agreement?
Is this established as the union: reality!
Relationship, trust, faith and promise.
Are these principles intrinsic or then what do you really ask of me?
If I have a dollar and your commitment,
What degree have you influenced me?
With that dollar and your commitment, I can buy a newspaper.
But, in the age of the internet I don't need a newspaper.
Now really, what are you asking of me?
The Person Who Would Be My god!

Bishop David Allen Hall- Public Saint

PRAISE

FAMILY UNITY

"Trust in the Lord with all thine heart: and lean not unto thine own understanding. In all thine ways acknowledge him, and he shall direct thy path." **Proverbs 3:5-6, KJV**

When things are going on, don't take part in negative activities.

Gloria Lang Gregory

PRAYER OF COMFORT

Throughout my entire life I found Comfort, Deliverance, and Peace whenever I've needed it! Especially Psalms Chapters 15 and 16. 15. "He will call upon me, and I will answer Him; I will be with him in trouble; l Will rescue him and honor him. 16. "With a long life I will satisfy him, And I will let him see my Salvation." **Psalm 91, KJV**

The entire Psalms 91 has always brought me peace and comfort throughout my life!!!! Now at 80 years of age, it brings comfort. And that Peace that is yet bringing me comfort!!! Amen.

Mary Carter Lang Payne

THANK YOU HEAVENLY FATHER

Dear Lord, my heavenly Father, first, I want to start by saying thank you for all of the good things you've done for my family and me and also for the not-so-good things you've bought me through. I never take anything for granted, like my health, my freedoms, my finances, or my family and friends. I realize that all of these are gifts from you.

I want to pray for all who may read this prayer, present and future, that they may come to a loving and saving relationship with you through your Son Jesus Christ! Though this life may be good now, it's nothing compared to the eternity you have planned for those who have placed their trust in you.

Thank you for all the patriarchs of our family who have paved the way for us and set forth a good example in conduct and deeds, so help the following generations to build a godly house on that foundation laid.

Let your angel of protection stand guard in our family. Let love and wisdom guide our decisions in life. May we never forsake your statutes and commandments, and if any should ever lose their way in this journey of life, may you restore them and guide them back to paths of righteousness with your love, grace, and everlasting mercy. AMEN!

Terrence Lamar Harvey

LOVE, THANKS, AND PRAISE

***"O God, thou art my God; early will I seek thee: my soul thirsteth for thee; my flesh longeth for thee in a dry and thirsty land, where no water is;"...*Psalm 63, KJV**

I love you, my family, no matter where you are or how far away you are. Please know that you are loved and prayed for.

First, let me say thanks to our family and saints that have gone before us.

Their prayers yet sustain us.

We have a love for our Lord and Savior in this family, and I don't see that nowadays! But, we have a thirst, a need for His word, Psalm 63. It is in our DNA!!!

The Most High God will see us through these times Psalms 35. Josh 1:9 says, "Be Strong and of a good courage for our Lord is with us and he fights for us!

I remember what and who has gone before us, and like them, "WE" must endure to the end! The Father loves his people, and we are the people of the Book! I know this family can see that playtime is over. Let us be ready, for the Bridegroom cometh!!!

All Praises to The Most-High God and His dear Son Jesus Christ!!!

Thank you, parents for your love and being the vessel God used to get us here and raising us in God's loving word.

La Rhonda Lang Turner

MY JOURNEY

***"Not everyone that saith Lord, Lord shall enter the kingdom of heaven, but he that doeth the will of my Father which is in heaven."* Matthew 7:21, KJV**

As I continue my personal journey with Christ, I will trust in the Lord.

Rachel Gregory

LOVE

"Love is patient, love is kind. It does not envy, it does not boast, it is not proud.

It is not rude; it is not self-seeking. It is not easily angered; it keeps no records of wrong.

Love does not delight in evil but rejoices with the truth. It always protects, always trusts.

Always hopes, always preserves. Love never fails…." 1 Corinthians 13:4-8

Explanation:

God's greatest gift to us was his only begotten son, Jesus. He never fails us, so let's not fail one another!

Family, I love you all and spread your love

Ivan Gregory

SEEKING GOD IN MY LIFE

Proverbs 3:5-6

Trust in the Lord with all thine heart and lean not unto your own understanding.

In all ways acknowledge him and he shall direct thy paths.

It was once my understanding that if I accepted Jesus as my Lord and Savior and confessed it openly that I was saved and would enter his kingdom. Wow was I wrong. I wanted a strong, powerful, and personal relationship with Christ.

The more I sought him, the more he revealed to me.

Gretta Gregory

EXPLANATION 1

Obeying God's vision will bring God's provision.

Explanation: When I do all the things God tells me to do, He does for me all the things that I can't do!!

Duncan Gregory

MY FAVORITE BIBLICAL PASSAGE

"For the Kingdom of Heaven is as a man traveling into a far country, who called his own servants, and delivered unto them his goods.

And unto one he gave five talents, to another two, and to another one; to every man according to his several; and straightway took his journey.

Then he that had received five talents went and traded with the same and made them other five talents.

And likewise, he that had received two, he also gained other two...

But he that had received one went and digged in the earth, and hid his Lord's money."

Matthew 25:14-18, KJV

Dr. Lorenzo Pitts, Jr.

HOLY COMMUNION PRAISE TO THE LORD

- The Lord's Supper is not only an expression of worship for believers, but by its very nature, it is evangelistic.
- In the Lord's Supper, the work of Christ is held up as an invitation for people to trust in the Lord.
- For believers, the Lord's Supper is an occasion for spiritual renewal and refocusing of kingdom priorities.

Elder Lewis Hall

SPECIAL BEDTIME BIBLE PASSAGE

"4 Love endures long *and* is patient and kind; love never is envious *nor* boils over with jealousy, is not boastful *or* vainglorious, does not display itself haughtily.

5 It is not conceited (arrogant and inflated with pride); it is not rude (unmannerly) *and* does not act unbecomingly. Love (God's love in us) does not insist on its own rights *or* its own way, *for* it is not self-seeking; it is not touchy *or* fretful *or* resentful; it takes no account of the evil done to it [it pays no attention to a suffered wrong].

6 It does not rejoice at injustice *and* unrighteousness but rejoices when right *and* truth prevail.

7 Love bears up under anything *and* everything that comes, is ever ready to believe the best of every person, its hopes are fadeless under all circumstances, and it endures everything [without weakening].

8 Love never fails [never fades out or becomes obsolete or comes to an end]."

1 Corinthians 13:4-8.

Lord, when everything is coming apart in my life, grant me the wisdom to ask you to please hold me together.

Elder Lewis Hall and Evangelist De Ella White Hall

EXPLANATION 2

"APRPBWPRAAAOA"

Explanation:

Affirmative Prayers Releases Powers By Which Positive Results Are Achieved And Or Accomplished.

Norman Vincent Peale

Duncan Gregory

AFFIRMATIONS, BLESSINGS, AND MEDITATIONS

TERRITORY

The act of claiming who you are as an individual is vital in trying to understand where you have been.

One of the most important things ever told to me …

> ***"doing the same thing over and over again***
> ***and expecting a different result is the definition of insanity".***

The veins, arteries, and capillaries in your body make up a distance of 60,000 miles,
enough to wrap around the earth twice.
Be elastic!
Poor circulation in the human body is like forced migration.
Causing people to become hardened, rerouted, and feeling isolated
creating slow and laborious work for the heart.
But our ancestors knew adaptability well.
It was their friend in incomprehensible times.
You are not alone.

Stay in a state of flux.
Changing, adapting, strengthening, learning, reassessing
claiming.
Two times around the earth,
that is the constant migration happening in your body.
Never let anyone take that away from you.

Writing this allowed me to reflect on what has felt like a very long, difficult, and rewarding journey even though,
in hindsight, it is just beginning.
Because now I am looking at my migration
my uncharted island
and seeing the bridges.

You might see yourself as different or not understood,
which might be the case,
but you are not alone.
Our family has been redefining itself for generations.
In the name of our ancestors
please allow yourself acceptance
until you feel full, abundant, and ready.

Take agency and ownership over our movement, our journey,
and pride in the way you walk it.
Claim territory over the 60,000 miles in your body.
A map of knowledge for survival and growth.
This migration is our sacred ritual,
Your witness makes it real.

Your Legacy,
Always be a reminder of your ancestry, understanding the
elasticity to the word.

Claude Edward Barnes

GOD'S BLESSINGS

May GOD our Creator's blessings be upon you, the Lang Watson Family. May He bless you with wisdom and humility. May He bless you with good health and longevity so that you may carry out the Plan He has for your life. May GOD's blessing protect you during your travels, whether near or far, coming home or departing. May His blessing be upon your beloved children as they seek to assimilate and find their way in an inhospitable and unsympathetic world. May His love for you be sufficient to sustain you during times of trouble or despair. In the morning, when you rise and feel the light on your face and the joy in your heart, just say thank you for blessing you with another day. GOD, we beseech you to Bless the Lang Watson family so that they may understand that their successes and accomplishments today are built on the foundation laid by their ancestors. Bless them so that they will know that you have given them *victory* over fear, a promising future, and family ties that bind and help to strengthen generations to come. In your name, I pray, Amen.

S. Claudia Lang Pitts

DAILY AFFIRMATIONS: MY TRUTH

1. I trust myself to make the best decision for me.
2. I am proud to be me.
3. I am blessed with an incredible family.
4. I choose to see the good in everyone.
5. I will learn something from everyone in my life.
6. I am grateful for all the love that surrounds me.
7. I will bounce back.
8. I am blessed to be safe.
9. I will use my resources.
10. I won't worry about things I can't control.

Jonathon Edward Barnes

MORNING OR BEDTIME MEDITATION

"Give ear to my words, O Lord, consider my meditation. Hearken unto the voice of my cry, my King, and my God: for unto thee will I pray. My voice shalt thou hear in the morning, O Lord; in the morning will I direct my prayer unto thee, and will look up..." Psalm 5:1-3

Take time (quiet time, to meditate and reflect on what God has done for you yesterday – last week - last year. Meditate on your current relationship with Him. Focus on whether your goals aligned with the path He has set forth for you. Concentrate on what you need from Him and make your specific request in accordance with His will for your life. Meditate on your affirmations.

To help you get started, repeat the words below in a slow humming sound:

YES, YES, YESS…. Yesss… Yessss…. Yesssss…

Yes Lord! Yes Lord! Yes Lord! Yes Lord! Yes Lord! Yes Lord!

Yes to your will. Yes to your will. Yes to your will. Yes to your will. Yes to your will. Yes to your will.

I need your help. I need your help. I need your help. I need your help. I need your help. I need your help.

We need you now! We need you now! We need you now! We need you now! We need you now! We need you now!

Thank you Lord. Thank Lord. Thank you Lord. Thank you Lord. Thank you Lord. Thank you Lord.

REPEAT

Pentecostal/Unknown

I have been young and now am old; Yet never have I seen the righteous forsaken, Nor his seed begging bread.

Psalm 37:25, King James Version

ACKNOWLEDGEMENTS

We acknowledge that without the encouragement and participation of Lang Watson family members, the publication of this book would not have been possible.We acknowledge and thank our ancestors who instilled in us the desire and need to pray to GOD, our Creator. Through prayer, our faith has become stronger, family ties strengthened, and our spiritual fellowship with church and community more satisfying.

On behalf of the Lang Watson Foundation, we are deeply grateful to the Prayerbook Project Committee for their tireless efforts in reaching out to family members, bringing creative ideas to the discussions, and remaining patient and optimistic about the project throughout the Coronavirus Pandemic Crisis. They struggled through numerous virtual Zoom meetings and saw this effort through to its completion.

Special thanks to committee members across the country: Mona L. Lampkin Barnes and Elder Claude Lang, co-chairs; and members Duncan Gregory, Leora Harvey Lockett, Curtis J. Pounds, and their support teams.We appreciate the support and creative freedom extended to us by the Lang Watson Foundation's Board of Directors.

We acknowledge and appreciate family members from youth to senior adults eighty-plus years, who shared their personal prayers, spiritual thoughts, meditations, poems, and affirmations for this publication.This legacy project is a collective effort of contributions from family members across the United States: Arizona, California, Colorado, Florida, Georgia, Illinois, Indiana, Minnesota, New York, Nevada, Ohio, Texas, Tennessee, and Virginia, as well as the United Kingdom. We thank you for your willingness to participate in this project and your permission to publish your work.We hope that this family "Book of Prayers, Praises, and Poems," a legacy project lives up to your expectation and remains a valuable family keepsake for generations to come.

Any errors or omissions in this book are unintentional.

INDEX

LANG WATSON FAMILY CONTRIBUTORS AND LINEAGE"

A Blessing and Prayer for the Righteous. Bishop John E. Lang, Sr., Paradise Temple Church, Pastor and Founder, Divine Agreement Fellowship, Paradise Vision of Hope Outreach Ministries Church. Illinois. Parents, Reverend Claude Lang and Hazel Watson Lang. Decedent of Wilson and Ada Leone Watson, Frederick and Annabelle Lang.

A Family Prayer. Mark R. Harvey, Georgia. Parents, Missionary Nancy Lang Harvey Samuels and Lawrence Bernard Harvey. Grandson of Rev. Claude and Hazel Watson Lang

A Mother's Prayer. De Edward and Carol Lang. Nevada. Parents Will and Mary Lang.

A Personal Prayer. Bishop David Allen Hall, Public Saint. Tennessee.

Affirmations of Prayer over our Children and Grandchildren. Bishop John E. Lang, Sr., Paradise Temple Church, Pastor and Founder, Divine Agreement Fellowship, Paradise Vision of Hope Outreach Ministries Church. Illinois

All Things Wonderful. Chani Ivy Weiss, Georgia. Parents, John Weiss and Elizabeth Magee Weiss

Bless My Family Prayer. Missionary Leora Harvey Lockett. Indiana. Parents, Missionary Nancy Lang Harvey Samuels and Lawrence Bernard Harvey.

Bedtime Prayer No. 1. Claudia Magee. Parent, Cassie Magee. Georgia. Granddaughter of Lisa Lampkin Magee.

Bedtime Prayer No. 2. Inez Love. Parent, Rachel Magee. Georgia. Granddaughter of Lisa Lampkin Magee.

Bedtime Prayer No. 3. Empress Love. Parents, Rachel Magee. Georgia. Granddaughter of Lisa Lampkin Magee.

Bedtime Prayer No. 4. Amanda Charles, Georgia. Parents, Patricia Charles and Mark Harvey.

Comfort and Peace. Elder Claude Lang. California. Parents, Bishop John E. Lang, Sr. and Mary Carter Lang Payne.

Cry Jesus. Missionary Nancy Lang Harvey Samuels. Indiana. Parents: Reverend Claude and Hazel Watson Lang. S. Decedent of Wilson and Ada Leone Watson, Frederick and Annabelle Lang.

COVID FREE. Mona LaRose Lampkin Barnes. Virginia. Parents, S. Claudia Lang Lampkin Pitts and Herbert Lampkin. Granddaughter of Rev. Claude and Hazel Watson Lang.

Daily Affirmation. Dr. Lorenzo Pitts, Jr., Georgia. Spouse, S. Claudia Lang Lampkin Pitts

Daily Affirmations: My Truth. Jonathon E. Barnes. Virginia. Parents, Mona LaRose Lampkin Barnes and Robert E. Barnes. Grandson of Claudia Lang Pitts and Herbert Lampkin, and great-grand son of Rev. Claude and Hazel Watson Lang.

Dear Dairy. Missionary Phyllis Yvonne Lang Adams. Indiana. Parents, Reverend Claude Lang and Hazel Watson Lang. Decedent of Wilson and Ada Leone Watson, Frederick and Annabelle Lang.

Deliverance. S. Claudia Lang Lampkin Pitts. Georgia. Parents, Reverend Claude and Mother Hazel N. Watson Lang, Decedent of Wilson and Ada Leone Watson, Frederick and Annabelle Lang.

Emotional Healing. Abbie Leona Tolbert, Imprfc Minister. Texas. Parents, Rev. Hallie Tolbert and Verna Leona Watson Tolbert

Explanation 1. Duncan Gregory. Minnesota. Parents, Gloria Lang Gregory and Alfred Gregory

Explanation 2. Duncan Gregory. Minnesota. Parents, Gloria Lang Gregory and Alfred Gregory

Faith Through Prayer. Shawnette Lang. California. Parents, Bishop John E. Lang, Sr. and Mary Carter Lang Payne.

Faithfulness. Patricia Ann Charles Harvey. Spouse, Mark Harvey

Family Daily! Crystal and Juan Flynn, Illinois. Parents, Roland Flynn and Myrtle Watson Flynn.

Family Unity: Gloria Lang Gregory, Indiana, daughter of the late Elder Claude and Sister Hazel Lang
Favorite Word. Joyce Hall Rice. Indiana. Submitted on behalf of her Mother Julia Ruth Watson Hall

For all the negatives things, God has Positive Answers. Pulpit Helps, Vol. 25, #3 March 2000. Joyce Hall Rice. Indiana. Submitted on behalf of her Mother Julia Ruth Watson Hall and Bishop Milton Hall.

Forgiveness and Praise. Marietta Hall. Indiana. Mother Joyce Hall, Grandparents Mother Julia Ruth Watson Hall and Bishop Milton Hall.

Glorification and Praise: Hazel Lang Mace. Indiana. Parents, Reverend Claude and Mother Hazel N. Watson Lang. Decedent of Wilson and Ada Leone Watson, Frederick and Annabelle Lang.

God's Angels. Gretta Gregory. Indiana. Parents. Gloria Lang Gregory and Alfred Gregory.

God's Blessings. S. Claudia Lang Lampkin Pitts. Georgia. Parents: Reverend Claude and Hazel Watson Lang. S. Decedent of Wilson and Ada Leone Watson, Frederick and Annabelle Lang.

God's Heart. Pastor Milton L. Hall, Jr, Grace Memorial COGIC. Indiana. Parents, Mother Julia Ruth Watson Hall and Bishop Milton Hall.

God's Plan. Kimberly Kimble and daughter Zori Kimble. Indiana. Parents Hazel Lang Mace and James Mace.

God of the Universe, Earth, Heavens, and All Men. Claudia M. Owens. Georgia. Parent, Paula Lampkin

Good Morning Lord. Dr. Joan A. Watson Ganns. Florida. Parents, Dr. James T. Watson and LeJeun E. Garnell Watson

Grateful. Curtis J. Pounds. Georgia. Parents Hazel Lang Mace and James Mace.

Here I Kneel. Mona LaRose Lampkin Barnes. Virginia. Parents, S. Claudia Lang Lampkin Pitts and Herbert Lampkin. Granddaughter of Rev. Claude and Hazel Watson Lang.

Holy Communion: Praise to the Lord. Elder Lewis Hall. Indiana. Parents, Mother Julia Ruth Watson Hall and Bishop Milton Hall.

In Your Name. Fredalyn Lang. Illinois. Parents, Bishop John E. Lang, Sr. and Gwendolyn Scoggins Lang

Intercessory Prayer for Loved Ones. Clara Phillips. New York. Descendant of Clora Lang

Intercessory Prayer for My Friend. S. Claudia Lang Lampkin Pitts. Georgia. Parents, Reverend Claude and Mother Hazel N. Watson Lang

It's Up to Me. Lawrence Lampkin, Georgia. Parent, Lisa Lampkin Magee.

Love. Ivan Gregory. Indiana. Parents, Gloria Lang Gregory and Alfred Gregory

Love One Another. Evangelist De Ella White Hall, Indiana. Spouse, Elder Lewis J. Hall

Love, Thanks, and Praise. La Rhonda Lang Turner. California. Parents, Bishop John E. Lang, Sr. and Mary Carter Lang Payne.

Miracles, Signs and Wonders. Evangelist De Ella White Hall, Indiana. Spouse, Elder Lewis J. Hall

Morning – Bedtime Meditation. S. Claudia Lang Lampkin Pitts. Georgia. Parents, Reverend Claude and Mother Hazel N. Watson Lang

My Daily Prayer. Bishop John E. Lang, Sr., Paradise Temple Church, Pastor and Founder, Divine Agreement Fellowship, Paradis Vision of Hope Outreach Ministries Church. Illinois

My Favorite Biblical Passage. Dr. Lorenzo Pitts, Jr. Spouse, S. Claudia Lang Lampkin Pitts

My God, Thank You. Ruth Lang. California. Spouse, Elder Claude Lang

My Gratitude to You. Juanice Petty. Indiana. Parent, Missionary Nancy Lang Harvey Samuels

My Journey. Rachel Gregory McLendon. Arizona. Parents, Gloria Lang Gregory and Alfred Gregory.

My Personal Relationship with God. S. Claudia Lang Lampkin Pitts, Georgia. Parents, Reverend Claude and Mother Hazel N. Watson Lang

My Prayer is... Smiley Lang. Nevada. Parents, Will Lang and Mary Johnson Lang.

My Prayer to God. Paster Emmanuel John. Indiana. Spouse, Missionary Theresa Harvey John

My Prayer to God for You. Missionary Theresa Harvey John

My Request. Bishop David Allen Hall, Public Saint. Tennessee.

My Strength. Lawrence Lampkin, Georgia. Parent, Lisa Lampkin Magee.

Our Special Bible Passage. Al and Carla Gregory. Illinois. Parents, Gloria Lang Gregory and Alfred Gregory.

Pray God is Listening. Missionary Leora Harvey Lockett. Indiana. Parents, Missionary Nancy Lang f and Lawrence Bernard Harvey.

Prayer for Covering. Bishop John E. Lang, Sr., Paradise Temple Church, Pastor and Founder, Divine Agreement Fellowship, Paradise Vision of Hope Outreach Ministries Church. Illinois. Parents, Reverend Claude Lang and Hazel Watson Lang

Prayer from the Heart. Elizabeth Hazel Magee Weiss. Georgia. Parents, Lisa Lampkin Magee and Leonard Magee.

Prayer of Comfort. Mary Carter Lang Payne. California

Prayer of Praise. Fredalyn Lang. Illinois. Parents, Bishop John E. Lang, Sr. and Gwendolyn Scoggins Lang

Prayers to Our Father in Jesus' Name. Bishop John E. Lang, Sr., Paradise Temple Church, Pastor and Founder, Divine Agreement Fellowship, Paradis Vision of Hope Outreach Ministries Church. Illinois. Parents, Reverend Claude Lang and Hazel Watson Lang

Roots of the Langs.' Rose Marie Lang-Everson. Missouri. Parents, Reverend Hoston and Rose Anna Lang. Decedent of Frederick and Annabelle Lang.

Scriptures to live by from my Mother. Debra Harvey Williams Lanham. Wisconsin. Parents, Missionary Nancy Lang Harvey Samuels and Lawrence Bernard Harvey.

Seeking God in My Life. Gretta Gregory. Indiana. Parents. Gloria Lang Gregory and Alfred Gregory.

Seeking You. Mona LaRose Lampkin Barnes. Virginia. Parents, S. Claudia Lang Lampkin Pitts and Herbert Lampkin. Granddaughter of Rev. Claude and Hazel Watson Lang.

Seeking You and Thanking You God. Curtis J. Pounds. Georgia. Parents Hazel Lang Mace and James Mace. Grandson of Rev. Claude and Hazel Watson Lang.

Self-Rejection. S. Claudia Lang Lampkin Pitts, Georgia. Parents, Reverend Claude and Mother Hazel N. Watson Lang. Decedent of Wilson and Ada Leone Watson, Frederick and Annabelle Lang.

Special Bedtime Bible Passage. Elder Lewis Hall and Evangelist DeElla White Hall. Indiana. Parents, Mother Julia Ruth Watson Hall and Bishop Milton Hall.

Submit to Guidance. Curtis J. Pounds. Georgia. Parents Hazel Lang Mace and James Mace. Grandson of Rev. Claude and Hazel Watson Lang.

Territory. Claude Edward Barnes. Scotland. Parents. Parents, Mona LaRose Lampkin Barnes and Robert E. Barnes, grandson of Claudia Lang Pitts and Herbert Lampkin, and great-grand son of Rev. Claude and Hazel Watson Lang.

Thank You. Talia Iris Weiss. Georgia. Parents, John Weiss and Elizabeth Magee Weiss. Granddaughter of Lisa Lampkin Magee and Leonard Magee

Thank You Heavenly Father. Terrance Lamar Harvey. Indiana. Son of Missionary Theresa Harvey John and great grandson of Rev. Claude and Hazel Watson Lang

Thankful. Lisa Lampkin Magee. Parents, Parents, S. Claudia Lang Lampkin Pitts and Herbert Lampkin. Georgia. Granddaughter of Rev. Claude and Hazel Watson Lang

The Peace of Your Best Self. Missionary Leora Harvey Lockett. Indiana. Parents, Missionary Nancy Lang Harvey Samuels and Lawrence Bernard Harvey.

The Person Who Would Be My God! Bishop David Allen Hall, Public Saint. Tennessee.

The Savior's Words. Joyce Hall Rice. Indiana. Submitted on behalf of her Mother Julia Ruth Watson Hall

Thoughts of Peace. Fredalyn Lang. Illinois. Parents, Bishop John E. Lang, Sr. and Gwendolyn Scoggins Lang

Watch Over Us. Love Barnes. Indiana. Daughter of Marietta Hall, Granddaughter, Joyce Hall Rice. Great Granddaughter Mother Julia Ruth Watson Hall and Bishop Milton Hall.

You Know Me Jesus. Curtis J. Pounds. Georgia. Parents Hazel Lang Mace and James Mace, Grandson of Rev. Claude and Hazel Watson Lang.

Your Personal Prayer of Forgiveness. Bishop John E. Lang, Sr., Paradise Temple Church, Pastor and Founder, Divine Agreement Fellowship, Paradise Vision of Hope Outreach Ministries Church. Illinois. Parents, Reverend Claude Lang and Hazel Watson Lang

WATSON – LANG
ANCESTRAL LINAGE

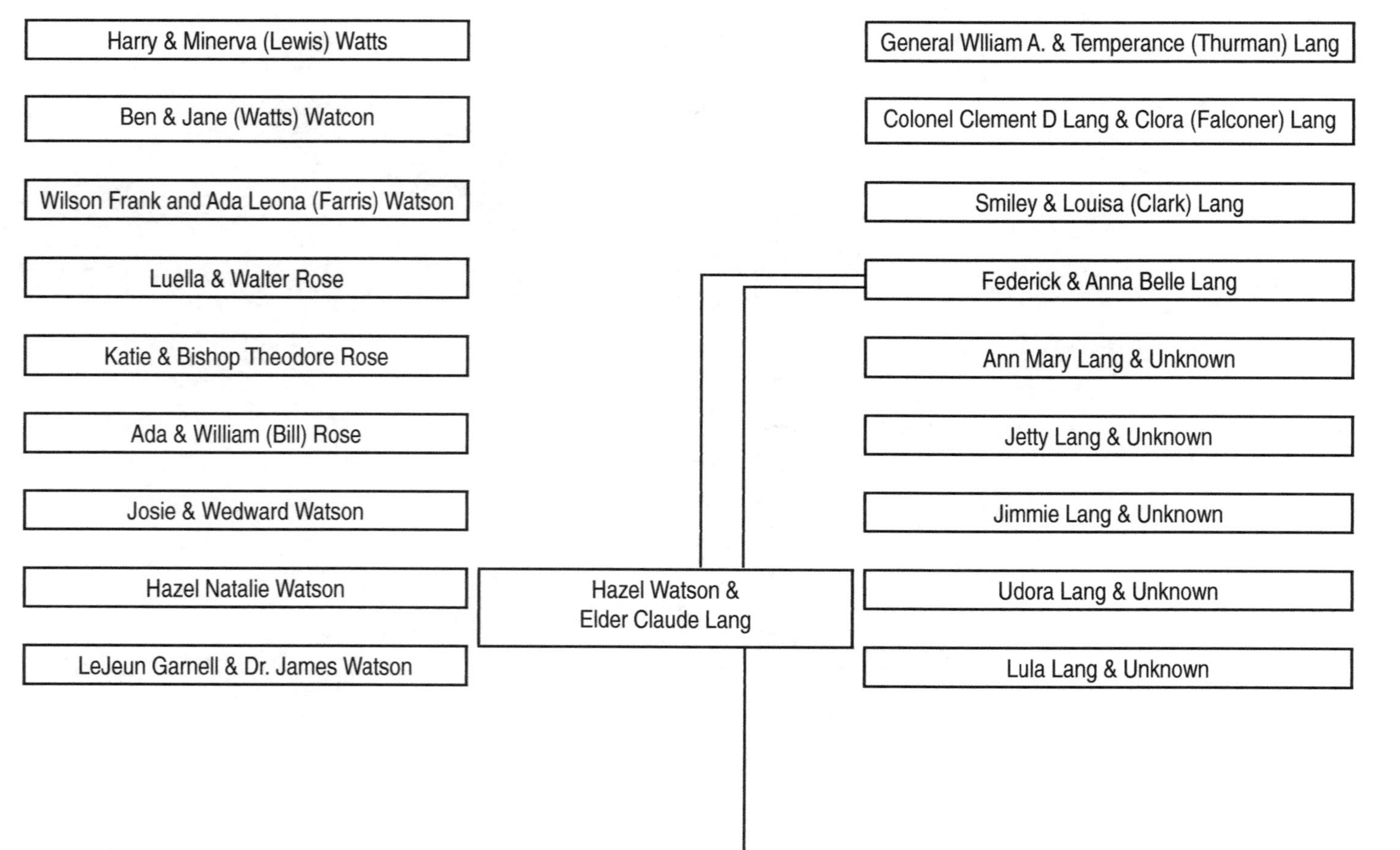
Harry & Minerva (Lewis) Watts
Ben & Jane (Watts) Watcon
Wilson Frank and Ada Leona (Farris) Watson
Luella & Walter Rose
Katie & Bishop Theodore Rose
Ada & William (Bill) Rose
Josie & Wedward Watson
Hazel Natalie Watson
LeJeun Garnell & Dr. James Watson
Hazel Watson &
Elder Claude Lang
General Wlliam A. & Temperance (Thurman) Lang
Colonel Clement D Lang & Clora (Falconer) Lang
Smiley & Louisa (Clark) Lang
Federick & Anna Belle Lang
Ann Mary Lang & Unknown
Jetty Lang & Unknown
Jimmie Lang & Unknown
Udora Lang & Unknown
Lula Lang & Unknown

Ruth Marguerite Jones & Albert Watson

Jewel & David Watson

Daisy Watson & Isaiah Johnson & Frank Cole

Cecil Watson - Unwed

Ruth Watson & Bishop Milton Hall

Myrtle Watson & Roland Flynn

Anna Rose Harris &
Elder Hoston Lang

Mary Johnson & Will Lang

Burrell Lang & Unknown

Earlean Lang & Grissett

Gertrude Lang & Unknown

Maggie Lang & Unknown

Will Lang

WATSON-LANG ANCESTRAL LINEAGE SYNOPSIS.

Watson Family

Harry and Minerva arrived in Jamestown, Virginia, about 1830 from the great continent of Africa and were sold to the Watts and the Lewis Plantations, respectively, in Pike County, Missouri. They later married and had three boys and seven girls. Daughter Mildred married Wesley Rose, and they had six boys and three girls. Their son, William Wesley Rose, married Ada Leone Ferris. Together they had three boys. William died while the boys were toddlers. Later, Ada married Wilson Frank Watson, William's cousin, son of Jane Watts (daughter of Harry and Minerva Watts), and her husband Ben Watson, who were parents of six boys and three girls. Together, Wilson and Ada had nine children, raising 12 children in total.

Lang Family

William A Lang Sr. was born in Wales in 1750. He came to America as a young man and married Phoebe Harrelson, and they settled in Chesterfield District of South Carolina. They had three boys and two girls. Their son General William A. Lang, Jr. married Temperance Thurman, and they settled in Langdale (Clark County), Mississippi. They had three boys and one girl. Their son Colonel Clement Davenport Lang, bachelor and Master of the Lang Plantation, and Clora Falconer Lang, a house servant, begot son Smiley Lang 1858. Smiley married Louisa Clark in 1876, and they had 12 children.

LANG WATSON FOUNDATION

ROMANS 8:38–39

Dear Diary: February 28, 2001

Read my Bible. Praying continually.

For I am persuaded, that neither death, nor life, nor angels, nor principalities, nor powers, nor things present, nor things to come, nor heights, nor depth, nor any other creature, shall be able to separate me from the love of God, which is in Christ Jesus our Lord.

Romans 8:38–39

Missionary Phyllis E. Y. Lang Adams

LANG WATSON FOUNDATION

Reverend Claude and Hazel Watson Lang Foundation Incorporation, dba the Lang Watson Foundation, is a non-profit domestic corporation incorporated in the State of Indiana and in accordance with Internal Revenue Service rules and regulations in 2014. The Foundation was founded five years after the death of Reverend Claude Lang at the age of 107 to honor the life ministry of evangelism, music, and humanitarian work of Reverend Lang, his wife, the late Hazel Natalie Watson Lang, and the Lang Watson family ancestors.

The Corporation is formed to support human achievement through the expansion of educational opportunities to make a positive difference in the lives of individuals and institutions who demonstrate a commitment to inspire, advocate, and elevate humanity's moral values, and to promote a better community. Founding Board of Directors:

S. Claudia Lang Pitts, President
Hazel Lang Mace, Treasurer
Missionary Nancy Lang Harvey Samuels
Bishop John E. Lang, Director
Gloria Lang Gregory, Director
Missionary Phyllis Lang Adams, Honorary Director

Website: langwatsonfoundation.org

REVEREND CLAUDE LANG

March 6, 1902 – March 11, 2009

Known as an Apostle in our time, Reverend Claude Lang was born to Fredrick and Annabelle Lang in (Clark County) Langsdale, Mississippi. Reverend Lang is a descendant of Smiley and Lou Clog Lang, his grandparents, and great grandfather Clement D. Lang. Claude migrated to the Northwest Indiana East Chicago area in 1928 and shortly thereafter, accepted Christ, was baptized, and renewed his spiritual relationship with God. A committed Christian, in 1929, Claude began 80 years of work as an evangelist under the stewardship of Mother Nancy Gamble. He was later ordained by Bishop William Roberts of Chicago, Illinois. He married Hazel Natalie Watson, an accomplished pianist of Harvey, Illinois, in 1932. Together they raised six biological children who joined them in their ministry. He was featured in the Church of God in Christ (COGIC) International Publication's Whole Truth Magazine for his Christian endeavors saving souls and pioneering work establishing churches in the Midwest, "Classique News Magazine Albany, New York, and received numerous recognitions and awards for a lifetime of evangelism and humanitarian service. He fellowshipped with Faith Temple COGIC until his passing.

HAZEL NATALIE WATSON LANG, PIANIST

May 1, 1907 – August 2, 1992

Hazel Natalie Watson was born to Wilson Frank Watson and Ada Leone Ferris Watson in (Cook County) Harvey, Illinois, on a farm, the oldest girl of eight boys and four girls. She blossomed into a lovely, talented, and amazing Christian woman of many gifts, including an accomplished pianist and scribe. On June 8, 1932, she married Claude Lang, an ordained minister and evangelist. They were married for 60 years until her death in 1992. She joined him in his evangelism ministry along with their six children. The children sang gospel music, and she played the piano. She was the pianist for Faith Temple Church of God in Christ (COGIC) in East Chicago, Indiana, for more than 35 years, where she played for services and the church choirs. Noted for her immeasurable love for children, she served as the Sunshine Band Youth Leader for Faith Temple, COGIC's Northern Indiana Jurisdiction, and the State for several decades. She received numerous recognitions for her humanitarian work in the Church and the community.

FOUNDING BOARD OF DIRECTORS

President
S. Claudia L. Lang Pitts

Bishop John Edward
Lang, Sr.

Missionary Ada Nancy Ruth
Lang Harvey Samuels

Gloria Annabelle Eunice
Carol Lang Gregory

Treasurer
Hazel LeJeune O'lda
Lang Mace

Missionary
Phyllis Earlene Yvonne
Lang Adams

"THE SOUL OF THE FAMILY"

Legacy Project Book Committee Members

Co-Chair
Mona La'Rose Lampkin
Barnes, Virginia

Co-Chair
Elder Claude Lang,
California

Missionary Leora Harvey
Lockett (BOD)
Indiana

Duncan Gregory
Minnesota

Curtis John Pounds
Georgia

Reference and Family Photos

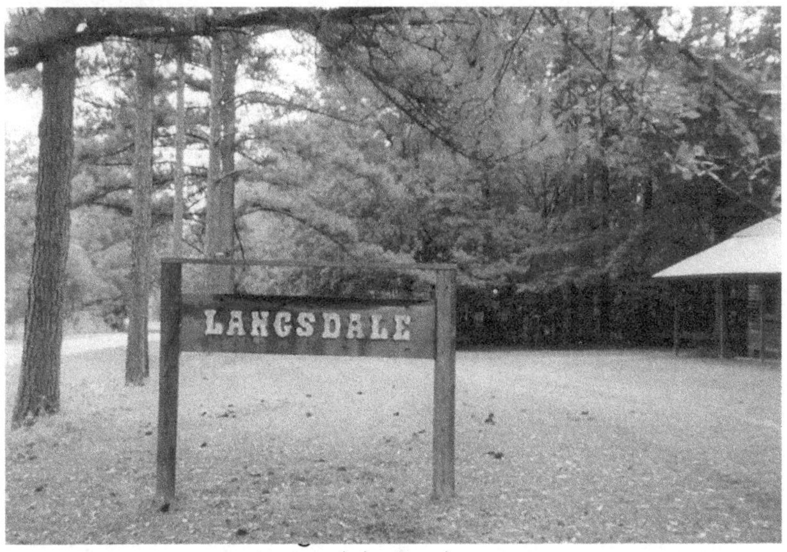

Langsdale Settlement
Clark County, Mississippi

"The Great House" 10,000 sq.ft. Antebellum architectural style house built and completed in 1855 by enslaved workers. Colonel Clement Davenport, owner; and biological father of Smiley Lang

Frederick Lang
(1881 – 1965)
Son of Smiley Lang and
Louisa Clark Lang

Louisa Clark Lang
(1820 – 1884)
Wife of Smiley Lang /
Mother of Frederick Lang

Rev. Claude Lang
(1902 – 2009)
Son of Frederick and
Annabelle Clark Lang
Married to Hazel
Watson 1932 to 1992

Hazel Natalie Watson Lang
Pianist
(1907 – 1992)
Daughter of Wilson
Frank and Ada Leone
(Ferris) Watson
Married to Rev. Claude
Lang 1932 to 1992

Rev. Hoston Lang
(1905 – 1978)
Son of Frederick and
Annabelle Clark Lang and
married to Rose Anna Harris

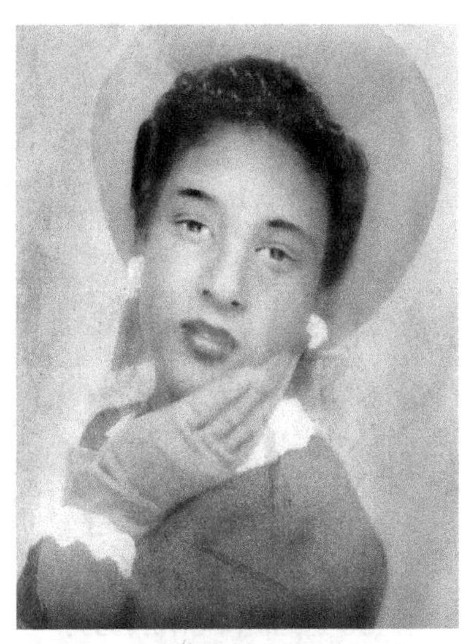

Beatrice Lang Jefferson
(1926 – 1950)
Daughter of Frederick and
Bessie Coleman Lang

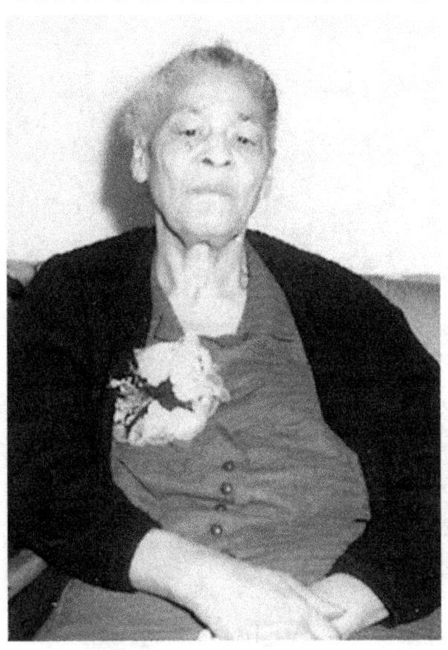

Earlean Lang Grissett
(1896 – 1977)
Daughter of Smiley Lang
and Louisa Clark Lang

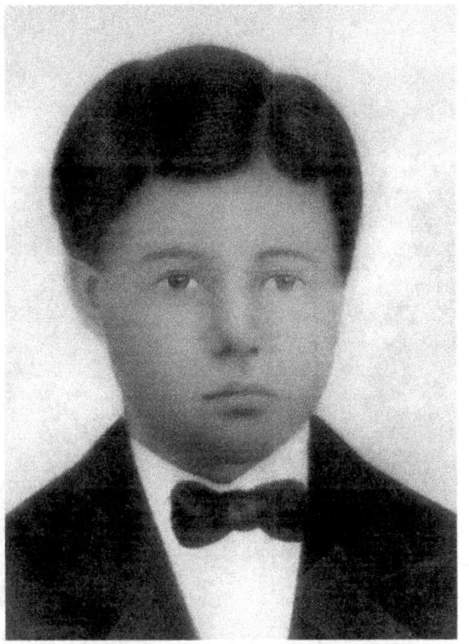

Will (Sugar Man) Lang
(1900 – 1983)
Son of Smiley Lang and
Louisa Clark Lang

Ada Leona Ferris Rose Watson (1882 – abt. 1963) Daughter of Taylor Ferris and Wife to William Wesley Rose and Wilson Frank Watson

Wilson Frank Watson (1882 – 1965) Son of Jane Watts Watson and Ben Watson, Husband of Ada Leona Farris Rose Watson

L to R Sons: Edward Watson, Cecil August Watson, David Watson, Bishop Theodore Rose (Watson), James Watson, Walter Rose (Watson), Albert Watson, and William (Bill) Rose (Watson) . Brothers gather after attending funeral services for their mother Ada.

Hazel Natalie Watson Lang – Pianist (1907 – 1992) Daughter of Wilson and Ada Watson and wife of Reverend Claude Lang

Reverend Claude and Hazel Natalie (Watson) Lang Married 1932 - 1992.

Ruth Julia Mae Watson Hall (1923 – 2019) Daughter of Wilson and Ada Watson and wife o Bishop Milton Hall for

Bishop Milton and Ruth Julia Mae (Watson) Hall Married (abt. 1942 - 2006)

Daisy Elizabeth Watson Johnson Cole (1919 - 1994) Daughter of Wilson and Ada Watson and wife of Isasiah Johnson and Frank Cole.

Bishop Theodore Rose (Watson) wife Kathy

Myrtle Katherine Watson Flynn (1925 – 2012) Daughter of Wilson and Ada Watson and wife of Roland Flynn for 70 + years

Roland and Myrtle Katherine (Watson) Flynn Married for 70+ years

Reverend Dr. James
Thomas Watson

Rev. Dr. James Thomas and
LeJeun E. (Garnell} Watson
Married 1936 - 1988

Deacon Albert
Wilson Watson
Son of Wilson Frank and
Ada Leona (Ferris) Watson

Deacon Albert Wilson
and Ruth Marguerie
Jones Watson
Married 1940 - 1992

NOTES

Favorite Scriptures

NOTES

Favorite Scriptures

NOTES

Favorite Scriptures

NOTES

Favorite Scriptures

NOTES

Favorite Scriptures

CPSIA information can be obtained
at www.ICGtesting.com
Printed in the USA
BVHW050747010622
637674BV00017B/61/J